Buddhist

Buddhist Meditation

IN THE SOUTHERN SCHOOL

THEORY AND PRACTICE
FOR WESTERNERS

BY

G. CONSTANT LOUNSBERY

B.SC., PRESIDENT OF LES AMIS DU BOUDDHISME

WITH A FOREWORD BY
W. Y. EVANS-WENTZ
M.A., D.LITT., D.SC. (OXON)

PILGRIMS PUBLISHING
◆ Varanasi ◆

BUDDHIST MEDITATION: In The Southern School
G. Constant Lounsbery

Published by:
PILGRIMS PUBLISHING

An imprint of:
PILGRIMS BOOK HOUSE
(Distributors in India)
B 27/98 A-8, Nawabganj Road
Durga Kund, Varanasi-221010, India
Tel: 91-542- 2314060, 2312456
E-mail: pilgrims@satyam.net.in
Website: www.pilgrimsbooks.com

PILGRIMS BOOK HOUSE (New Delhi)
9 Netaji Subhash Marg, 2nd Floor
Near Neeru Hotel, Daryaganj, New Delhi 110002
Tel: 91-11-23285081 Fax: 91-11-23285722
E-mail: pilgrim@del2.vsnl.net.in

Distributed in Nepal by:
PILGRIMS BOOK HOUSE
P O Box 3872, Thamel, Kathmandu, Nepal
Tel: 977-1-4700942, Off: 977-1-4700919
Fax: 977-1-4700943
E-mail: pilgrims@wlink.com.np

First Published 1936
Copyright © 2005, Pilgrims Publishing
All Rights Reserved

Cover design by Asha Mishra

ISBN: 81-7769-346-8

Printed in India at Pilgrim Press Pvt. Ltd. Lalpur Varanasi

PREFACE TO THE NEW EDITION

There have been many books written about both Buddhism and Meditation, and many dwell in detail on the facts and theories of the subjects. But there are far fewer titles which actually deal exactly with the methods of doing the meditations associated with Buddhism.

In this book the eminent writer on things Tibetan and Buddhist, W.Y. Evans-Wentz, adds his own thoughts on the subject matter. Evans Wentz is an anthropologist and he spent some years in the Himalayas, particularly in Kashmir/Ladakh, Garhwal and Sikkim. He himself has produced several books on Tibetan traditions, the Tibetan Yogi Milarepa, and Tibetan Yoga. He has clearly discussed the key features of this book and he leaves us little reason to add much more.

Suffice to say that the author, G. Constant Lounsbery has set out the various methods, which fine-tune the mind to meditation. He has succinctly encapsulated the differing exercises and methods one needs to learn in order to achieve some success in this most difficult and often baffling of practices.

The lessons of Buddhist Meditation in this book, first published in 1936, are as true today as they were when the ideas were first put to press. By following the procedure outlined here one can seek a higher clarity and rejuvenate one's whole being.

Bob Gibbons
Siân Pritchard-Jones
Kathmandu 2004

Even as the smith refines silver,
so gradually, little by little, moment after moment,
does the wise man fine away his defilements.

Dhammapada 239

FOREWORD

By W. Y. Evans-Wentz, M.A., D. Litt., D.Sc. (Oxon), Member of Jesus College, University of Oxford

THE SCIENCE OF BUDDHIST MEDITATION

Most treatises on Meditation and Yoga so far published in the Occident are chiefly expository, in a philosophical or historical way, rather than practical. But here, within these covers, we have, at last, a treatise which presents the essential technique and methods of meditation in its Buddhistic form so clearly and simply that any person of average intelligence desirous of practising such meditation can do so without difficulty, without danger, and without recourse to a *guru*. In Hindu and other systems of meditation and Yoga, on the contrary, particularly where certain breathing-exercises are prescribed, a *guru* is not only necessary to teach and to direct, but also to safeguard the *yogin*.

In commending this unique contribution to the advancement of learning made by Miss G. Constant

Lounsbery, President of Les Amis du Bouddhisme, Paris, I can do no better than to employ as my text the words of the Enlightened One, the Master of Meditation, the Buddha Gotama: "Without Knowledge there is no Meditation; without Meditation there is no Knowledge; and he who hath both Knowledge and Meditation is near to Reality."

In order to comprehend the significance of these words of the Buddha, it is necessary, first of all, to take into account some of the more outstanding views concerning man and the Universe which are in large measure peculiar to Buddhism.

Firstly, Buddhism, unlike the three Semitic faiths, Judaism, Christianity, and Islam, teaches that the sorrow of the world, being the direct *karmic* outcome of man's own actions, can be overcome only by man himself and not through the intervention of a Supreme Deity. In other words, man, having made himself and his worldly environment precisely what they are, must himself remake and then transcend them, by treading the Path of the Higher Evolution, which has been trodden and demarcated by those, like the Buddhas, who have gone ahead and become the Guides of Humanity.

Secondly, Buddhism emphasizes that the realization of Truth is incomparably more important than belief in Truth; that religious faith and devotion, being merely the first steps on the Path, are of themselves not enough; that if Truth is to be realized, there must be Right Belief, Right Intentions, Right Speech, Right Actions, Right Means of Livelihood, Right Endeavouring, Right Mindfulness, Right Meditation.

Thirdly, Buddhism distinguishes a higher or supramundane Wisdom, which differs fundamentally from Dogmatic Theology. And it is in virtue of having arrived at this Wisdom, or Right Knowledge, that the devotee transcends the lowly human state of existence and attains Emancipation from Sorrow and Complete Enlightenment.

According to Bhikkhu Parawahera Vajirañāṇa Thero, of the Theravādin school, the Buddha realized Reality, attained Final Release (known in Pāli as *Nibbāna* and in Sanskrit as *Nirvāṇa*), by means of Right Meditation; and by Right Meditation there is produced that purity and mastery of mind which lead to inner illumination.

In the Pāli Canon, Buddhist Meditation is called *Bhāvanā;* and this is the term to describe it which is most popular in the Theravādin, or Southern school. Of *Bhāvanā*, which implies systematic training of the mind, there are two stages: namely, *Samādhi-Bhāvanā* (which is preliminary), and *Vipassanā-Bhāvanā*. In the former, the meditator attains mental fixity, or one-pointedness of mind; is unaffected by the stimuli born of sensuous objects; and enjoys internal quiescence. In the latter, he attains intuitive vision of Reality. It is by these two methods that one arrives at Right Understanding and Right Knowledge.

As Miss Lounsbery's treatise on Buddhist meditation sets forth, there are forty objects for use in practising *Bhāvanā;* when adequate progress has been made, there is no longer dependence upon external objects in arriving at mental concentration, and the meditation becames wholly subjective. Then, the mind having become thoroughly purified and disciplined and all sensuousness having been transcended, there dawn the Four Ecstatic States, which Buddhism calls the Four *Jhānas.*

The Four *Jhānas* correspond to four stages progressively reached as a result of success in the practice of *Samādhi-Bhāvanā.* In the fourth or highest stage, one experiences transcendental blissful and complete tranquillity of body and mind. In that condition one is able to exercise the Five *Abhiññās,* which are profound intellectual attainments synonymous with the *Siddhi* of the *Yogins.* These are classified as (1) miraculous (or supernormal) accomplishments (or powers), (2) divine vision (or clairvoyance), (3) divine hearing (or clairaudience), (4) memory of previous births, and (5) insight into the mental processes, or thoughts, of others.

The aspirant who desires to develop the meditation further than this should meditate upon formless or purely mental objects. These are called *Arūpa-vacara*. By this means he reaches the four bodiless states of existence known as the *Arūpa-lokas*, which, however, like the Five Abhiññās, are neither to be striven after nor clung to if attained, for they are not the True Goal.

The candidate for *Nibbāna*, having reached the Fourth *Jhāna*, should next turn his mind toward *Vipassanā-Bhāvanā*, or Intuitive Meditation. Thereby he will come to understand intuitively the Three Characteristics of Conditioned Existence, which are transitoriness, sorrowfulness, and the voidness (or illusiveness) of all phenomenally existing things constituting the Cosmos. Then he should proceed to cultivate the Thirty-five Principles of Knowledge, known as *Bodhi-pakkhiya Dhamma*. By success in this practice, his mind becomes freed from every attachment to *sangsāric* (or karmically conditioned) existence; the Happiness of *Nibbāna* is won. This alone is the True Goal of all Buddhist Meditation.

Thus by introspective analysis of the psychic content of one's own mind, together with profound meditation-examination of each of the complex elements and activities which constitute sensuousness (or *sangsāric* consciousness) in its manifold expres-

sions, man comes to know himself in the sense taught
by the Great Mysteries of Ancient Egypt and Greece.
In other words, Meditation is the royal highway to
man's understanding of himself—of all the innumer-
able *karmic* predilections resulting in mental impulses
and actions both "good" and "evil," and of the whole
of sensuous being in the many worlds of the *Sangsāra*,
or Universe of Life's Dominion. This method is, however, to be differentiated from that of the psycho-
analyst, who analyses some other person's mind rather
than his own.

When by these means man attains to Right Knowledge, he sees with clear vision the cause and the cure
of the unsatisfactoriness of every conditioned state
of Beings, in heavens, hells, purgatories, and worlds;
he is enabled to value, at their true worth, all the
things of this world; and, like an adult who has out-
grown the playthings of childhood, no longer do the
troubles of the passion-fettered and pleasure-seeking
multitude interest him. Like one standing on the
summit of a mountain, he looks down on the domain
of transitoriness and suffering; he has transcended
every attachment to *sangsāric* existence. He has
emerged from the darkness of the Cave of Ignorance
and rejoices in the light of the Sun of Understanding.
No more will he enter the Cave; he has burst asunder
the cocoon of *karma*, which he himself had spun dur-

ing uncountable cycles of repeated birth and death; he is emancipated.

But, as he looks out over the Sea of Life, there arises, from the depths of his innermost consciousness, an overwhelming desire to descend once more to the Plane of Earth that he may point out to his fellow human beings the Path of Light, even as it has been pointed out throughout the æons by the Great Ones who have entered the Portal of the Higher Evolution and taken the Vow of the *Bodhisatva*. Or, as the Tibetan Sages teach us, "after having attained Liberation, there cometh infinite compassion for all those sentient beings who have not as yet recognized the true nature of their own mind."

And in like manner may everyone who enters upon the Way of Buddhist Meditation, as set forth in this volume, come to realize the promise conveyed by the words of the Enlightened One and thus attain the *Nirvāṇic* Goal.

W. Y. EVANS-WENTZ

Jesus College, Oxford
1935

PREFACE

BY THE AUTHOR

THE growth of interest in Buddhism must be obvious to any keen observer of the trend of thought.

The Orient is taking stock of the treasures of the Teaching and clearing it of those racial superstitions which have obscured the Essential Ideas of the doctrine. These racial or local superstitions are the result of the triumphal march of Buddhism across Asia through Ceylon, Burma, Siam, China, Japan, and Tibet. But the survival, through the centuries, of the Teaching seems to be due to the fact that *it imposes no dogma*.

The true Buddhist is a free thinker, a pioneer in search of truth, a compassionate, tolerant pioneer who seeks to disarm the one enemy: Ignorance. He is self-dependent, his own free intelligence must lead him toward his recompense—Supreme Knowledge and Insight, which is the fruit of meditation. For it is only through meditation that the Dhamma (the Doctrine) is understood thoroughly.

Free spiritual research is the one great adventure

for all who are discouraged by the failure of material-
ism and the burden of imposed dogmas.

Many excellent books upon Buddhism are avail-
able, but the simple instructions that are given in the
East by Guru to Chela, teaching him the necessary
physical and mental approach to meditation (according to Buddhist tradition), are difficult to come upon.

A method of mind-training is necessary, and this
method must be adapted to the mentality of modern
men; moreover, it must avoid the pitfalls and dangers
of certain occult practices.

When experience has been gained, the student will
no longer need to follow preliminary instructions and
practice-plans; he will be able to practise the purely
Buddhist meditations that are given in the latter part
of the book.

Profound gratitude is tendered to all the Bhikkhus,
and lay authorities upon meditation, who, in Ceylon
and in Europe, have graciously offered advice and
instruction.

The writings of the Bhikkhus Nyānatiloka Thero,
Nārada Thero, Parawahera Vajirañāṇa Thero, and
Bhikkhu Sīlācāra are frequently quoted in these
pages.

The Samaṇa Mahinda, a hermit meditating in the
forests of Ceylon ("a forest-dweller"), contributed the
plan of the Meditation upon Peace, especially de-

signed for Western students.

Special thanks are due to Dr. Cassius Pereira for his practical instructions included in the chapter on Concentration, and also for his explanation of the Meditation upon Breath Ānāpāna Sati).

I have availed myself of Dr. B. E. Fernando's study of the Four Fundamentals of Attentiveness. The Hon. Secretary of Les Amis du Bouddhisme, Mme M. La Fuente, has been of the greatest help in compiling this book and in controlling the numerous quotations and references.

Several of the most important subjects of meditation, scattered here and there through the Pāli Suttas, have been included in Part II. It is hoped that the explanations in the text will permit any serious student to understand the practice of concentration.

Meditation, the highest and the most important step upon the Path, must be practised very seriously; it was never meant for intellectual delectation. Its benefits are manifold—"One becomes that which one meditates."

> "May All Beings be Happy,
> May they be Peaceful."

G. C. L.

Paris
June 1935–2479

CONTENTS

PART I

THE THEORY OF MEDITATION

1

GENERAL OUTLINE

BUDDHISM is an "ethico-philosophical system" known in the East as the Dhamma, the Law, the Teaching of the Buddha Gotama. Its aim is Deliverance from *the Suffering which characterizes all phenomenal existence.* With this end in view, a very definite method of physical and mental training has been elaborated. By living a pure life (causing no harm to any living being), by cultivating intelligence, reasoning from cause to effect, intuitive thinking also is awakened. The Theravādin school insists that right living is absolutely necessary for the practice of right meditation.

Meditation is the eighth step on the path that leads to liberation. The Buddha did not impose a dogma, he pointed out the road that he himself (as well as all other Buddhas) had followed. The Buddhas only blaze a path through the jungle of ignorance, they point the way that leads to Nibbāna, beyond suffering. Free investigation and reason must guide each one upon the path.

Following the law of causality link by link, one arrives at:

1. The cessation of inferior states of consciousness;

2. The creation of superior states of consciousness, says the Bhikkhu P. Vajirañāṇa Thero.

Each man is the result of his thoughts in the past, and his present thoughts will condition his future lives. For a deed depends upon a thought; it is, in fact, only the manifestation of thought. A pure peaceful thought cannot give birth to a deed of violence.

It is quite possible to control and to purify thought; control is acquired through proper training in concentration.

When the mind has been sufficiently purified, it perceives the difference between the real values and the false or apparent values (of things), for reality is usually obscured by appearances.[1]

The aspirant for meditation sets out to conquer Supreme Knowledge. He must ever and again fortify and sustain his resolution by the practice of Morality (Sīla).[2] The control of the senses facilitates mind-control and vice versa; both must be cultivated simultaneously.

[1] That which appears to be true is unreal (it seems real to us because of our ignorance). Absolute truth (so unreal to the unenlightened) is realized by the wise man as the *only* Reality.

[2] Morality (Sīla)—Harmlessness (Ahiṃsa)—is one of the most important moral precepts of Buddhist and of Hindu morality.

When the senses and the mind are tranquillized and controlled, the disciple will be able to free himself from certain prejudices due to the habit of considering all things from a personal point of view. The obsession of separativity, the habit of setting up a "Self" in opposition to "Others," the "I consciousness," prevents impersonal thinking.

To obtain *true* Knowledge, it is absolutely necessary to think impersonally. In order to accomplish this, the student must follow a definite system of mind-training; he must plan out and practise certain exercises in order to obtain concentration. If he has a capacity (is apt) for meditation, the repeated practice of concentration will create a habit of mind.

Attentiveness

Before attempting to practise concentration the student should begin by training himself to observe attentively all that is going on around him. Let him try to observe the phenomena of life *impersonally*. He should then observe himself and study the workings of his body and his mind. Let him observe his gestures, his sentiments, his thoughts. Let him also try to find out the motive and the import of his every act.

This introspection should not become morbid; the student must scrutinize himself just as he would scrutinize the motives and actions of any other person.

Keen attentiveness should become a habit to be cultivated all through life.

Right Attentiveness is the seventh step on the Path and prepares the disciple for Right Meditation (the eighth step). "Buddhism is only one thing—Intelligence," said the Nāyaka of Asgiriya, overlord of this famous Kandyan monastery.

By systematically cultivating intelligence, ignorance will sooner or later be destroyed. It is ignorance that keeps alive selfish desires and blind attachments to sense objects. Such desires produce worried, troubled, and agitated states of mind, which must be stilled before one can meditate.

Subject

When the student has acquired the habit of keen Attentiveness, he should examine the forty classic subjects of meditation (Chapter 5), and choose a subject suitable to his character and to his occupations (*vide* Chapter 6).

Meditating upon a *suitable* subject, the student will decrease the power of inferior thoughts and tendencies—he will also increase the power of his higher thoughts and tendencies; for

Meditation Modifies Character

It will readily be seen that the choice of a subject

of meditation is important. The student should know whether anger, greed, avarice, etc., are dominating his nature. He must choose a subject that is contrary to the demeritorious tendencies of his character.

Interest

The subject chosen must also *interest* the student; an interesting subject will not make access to concentration too difficult.

Preparation

A physical and mental preparation for meditation is necessary. This preparation is described in Chapter 8, as are also certain breathing-exercises which calm the mind and help to banish (temporarily) the hindrances to meditation. These hindrances are wrong states of mind which interfere with meditation and even make it impossible to obtain real concentration.

When the student has followed these instructions, he will be prepared to concentrate upon a chosen subject of meditation.

Analysis

When the attention has been concentrated upon a certain subject, every other idea or thought foreign to the subject should be excluded. The student must examine and analyse the subject of meditation. Other thoughts will trouble his mind; this must not surprise him; he should not pay attention to these intruding thoughts; as far as possible he should ignore their presence.

Repetitive Thinking

If they persist let him substitute *"repetitive thinking"* for *"consecutive thinking."* For instance, if the subject of meditation is Peace, the student should repeat the word Peace . . . Peace . . . Peace, until it reverberates in his mind. By so doing all troublesome thoughts will be chased away.

The student must not tire his body or his mind. He must not strain his attention.

It will be necessary to begin the meditation all over again or to put it off (for the time being) if he is unable to concentrate.

Reflection

When attention has been concentrated and the subject of meditation has been analysed or examined thoroughly, the student should reflect upon all he has learned through analysis.

The subject of meditation must be one that *interests* the student *prodigiously,* for he must become absorbed in it. This absorption in an idea will soon lead to one-pointedness of mind.

Intuitive Thinking

After this, intuitive thinking will start functioning. Then a sense of joy and of well-being is experienced by the student, for he knows that he is approaching the plane of Pure Thought. He will be able very soon to discard all "verbal thoughts." He will not need words any longer, for intuition permits him to contact Peace. The thought of Peace will have penetrated his whole being. *The meditator and the subject of meditation become identified.*

Superior and subtler states of consciousness are gained in this way.

Clearly conscious, the student should develop the subject of meditation, enlarging the range of Peace until it includes the whole world of beings.

The calm, penetrating thought, acquired in meditation, will last over for some time. After the meditation is finished, the student should keep in mind all that he has experienced in meditation hours and reflect upon it.

It must not be forgotten that the habit of attentive observation should be cultivated at all times, as this will make concentration easier.

For his own happiness and for the happiness of all beings the life of a Buddhist should become "one long meditation." The true disciple radiates thoughts of boundless goodwill and loving-kindness toward all beings who suffer through ignorance.

Growth

A child, a man, and a sage see life differently. Even so the experiences of meditation will *gradually* and *repeatedly* cause the disciple to modify and to change his ideas. He must follow that which seems true to him at any given moment.

To determine whether a thought or act is pure, the Buddhist asks himself: "Will this diminish or increase suffering for me or any other being?" Anything that increases suffering is harmful to him, as well as to others. *He should not be the slave of habits of thought*. His mind should be free to accept the new ideas which his intelligence perceives, as it is increased and purified by meditation.

It may be said that the theory of Buddhist Meditation is that meditation modifies mind and therefore purifies life;[1] it also increases intelligence as well as compassion. It is therefore of great benefit to the whole world.

---

[1] The Zen sect of the Mahāyāna school is sometimes called the Sudden school, because it believes in a sudden flash of enlightenment (Satori). The work of purification must necessarily have been going on for some time before this is experienced.

2

ESSENTIAL IDEAS

BEFORE attempting to study Buddhist Meditation, it is necessary to have understood the essential ideas of the teaching (Dhamma).

Certain ideas are to be found in every Buddhist sect, whether of the Northern (Mahāyāna) or of the Southern (Theravāda) school.

Buddhism does not impose any dogma. The Buddhist must not accept any idea upon oral or written tradition. He must only believe that which he himself has proved to be true. Faith must *follow* the dictates of reason. He must be his own guide, *the Light is within him.* His vision, at any given moment, is determined by and depends upon the nature, the characteristics, and the tendencies created by his thoughts in the past. His future vision will depend upon the thoughts and actions of his present existence. Ignorance diminishes as thought is purified. He can re-create his life and raise his consciousness, for "Life is a Becoming"; it is not static, but dynamic. Moreover, as Knowledge increases, the Light (Bodhi),[1] *deeply* hidden within, will shine forth more clearly.

The Buddhas, the Enlightened Ones, only point out the way which each disciple must follow, proving to himself the Truth of the Teaching. The Teaching is lost periodically as men turn away from the Law, which each Buddha proclaims anew to his epoch, even as every other Buddha has proclaimed it in his day.

Supreme Knowledge (Bodhi) is latent in each man. "The Essence of mind is pure," as the Chinese Buddhists say. Selfish thoughts, carnal thoughts, which are born of greed, give birth in turn to hatred and to the idea of separativity. They weave a veil of ignorance that obscures the inner light.

All forms of life are interdependent, but man will set up a "Self," in opposition to all other beings, although all Life is one.

The Buddhist in his quest for wisdom will be guided by reason and knowledge rather than by sentiment or emotion. He must unravel the web of ignorance; he must hold fast to that which he has already proved true, and continue his search for Reality. Meditation will increase the capacity of his intellect and hasten his spiritual evolution.

"One thing only do I make known—Suffering and

1 The light of Supreme Knowledge.

Deliverance from Suffering."

"Even as the whole sea is impregnated with only one savour, that of salt, so, O disciples, this doctrine and this discipline are impregnated with one savour only, the savour of deliverance." (Culla Vagga.)

To abstain from that which is evil (that is, from creating suffering).

To do good.

To purify the heart.

This is the Teaching of all the Buddhas, and the essence of Buddhism.

It is meditation that helps the disciple to obtain purification and deliverance, if he is willing to lead a life that is pure and harmless to all beings.

Suffering is inextricably bound up with Life. The word Dukkha, translated "Suffering," has a wide range of meaning. It includes every state of physical or mental irritability, dissatisfaction, pain, or "dis-ease" of Body and Mind.

To prove this basic idea of Buddhism, it is only necessary to observe nature attentively. The ferocious struggle for existence can be verified easily. Man systematically destroys animals (for greed or gain) and cunningly contrives war against his fellow-man. In this struggle for life, suffering is always present (in one form or another), hidden or revealed. The victor as well as the victim will be overcome, sooner or later, by Sickness, Old Age, and Death. These are the messengers of Yama.

Buddhism has often been called pessimistic because of the keen, profound observation of life which has led to insistence upon the fact of suffering.[1] If a physician diagnoses a certain disease in a patient and prescribes a remedy that will certainly cure the disease, his diagnosis cannot be called pessimistic. This, however, would be true if there were no possible cure for the malady.

The Buddhist looks upon life fearlessly and sees it *"as it really is"* (Yathābhūta)—conditioned by Impermanence and Suffering. He knows that by his own efforts, with the help of his intelligence and of his compassion, he will be able to free himself, and help others to free themselves, from suffering.

There are three groups of Essential Ideas which should be considered; they can only be comprehended by the help of meditation. It is best to enumerate these groups and then to study each group in detail.

1. THE FOUR NOBLE TRUTHS

Concerning suffering, its cause and its destruction.

[1] Seeing suffering in all things, the Buddhist cultivates boundless compassion and tolerance.

II. THE THREE CHARACTERISTICS

of phenomenal existence: (1) Impermanence; (2) Suffering; (3) the Absence of any fixed (or unchanging) self (attā).

III. THE LAW OF CAUSALITY

Every cause is the result of an anterior cause and produces an effect which in its turn will be the cause of an effect.

The observation of this law as it operates in the Universe gave rise to the doctrine of Paticcasamuppāda [1] (causal origination), called the Chain of Causation. The first link of this chain ("the root of all existence") is Ignorance, and the last is Suffering. This law helps one to understand the causes of existence and the *Kamma* (action and reaction) which has conditioned one's present life.

THE THREE CHARACTERISTICS

Existence is characterized by:

1. Impermanence (Anicca);
2. Suffering (Dukkha);

---

1 (1) Ignorance; (2) Mental activities; (3) Consciousness; (4) Name and Form (Individuality); (5) The Six Organs of Sense; (6) Contact; (7) Feeling; (8) Craving; (9) Attachment or Clinging to Existence, in this world or another; (10) Process of Becoming; (11) Rebirth; (12) Old Age, Death, Sorrow, or Suffering. Each link gives rise to the next link in the chain.

3. And the fact that there is no fixed entity, no unchanging "Self," to be found in anything (Anattā).

It is only through deep meditation that these characteristics of existence can be thoroughly understood.

Anicca

Impermanence. Everything in the Universe is in a perpetual state of flux, changing at every moment. Impermanence may readily be observed; it is one of the causes of suffering, since man clings to that which is ever "on the wing." All happiness is fugitive. The Buddhist seeks to escape from *all impermanent states*.

Dukkha

Suffering, as has just been explained, is inherent in all phenomenal life. Its origin lies in ignorance (nescience), the desires born of ignorance, and attachment to these desires.

Anattā

Egolessness. Everything that composes personality is impermanent; sensations, emotions, thoughts, are ever changing. One is never the same during any two consecutive moments.

"Of that which is impermanent, subject to suffering, subject to change; how is it possible to say this is *my Self?*"

Corporeal form (Rūpa) is not the Self.

Sensation (Vedanā) is not the Self.

Perception (Saññā) is not the Self.

Mental activities (Sankhārā) are not the Self.

Consciousness (Viññāṇa) is not the Self.

In any one of these constituents, or aggregates of personality (whether taken separately or collectively), there is nothing permanent that may be called the "Self."

The meditation upon the Four Fundamentals of Attentiveness will help one to understand the impermanence of personality.

Anattā is conditioned by Anicca. That which man calls his personality or Self (attā) is just as impermanent as the external phenomena of the Universe, where the process of becoming is more easily observed.

It is *Continuity* that gives one the impression of possessing a permanent "Self." "Personality resembles a river whose waters are renewed incessantly." It is because change is possible that one can deliberately modify one's nature and improve it.

The Buddhist, seeing impermanence in all things around him (and also in all that makes up his personality), seeks deliverance from change and suffering upon the transcendental plane of Nibbāna. In meditating he first experiences that peace which is a foretaste of perfection.

Anicca	Anattā	Nibbāna
Impermanence	Egolessness	The state beyond desire

have been called the three cardinal principles of Buddhism.

He who understands impermanence should be able to understand Anattā later on. When the Anattā doctrine is realized, selfishness and personal vanity are destroyed.

Impermanence, Harmlessness, and the transcendental peace of Nibbāna are important ideas in Hindu philosophy also. But Hindu Nirvāṇa (Sanskrit) is not quite the same as Buddhist Nibbāna. The difference lies in the Buddhist idea of the Self (attā) as constantly changing—*Becoming* rather than *Being*. This doctrine is a raft whereby one may escape the limitations of personality. It is the keystone of Buddhism.

THE FOUR NOBLE TRUTHS

These four Truths were proclaimed by the Buddha in his first sermon. They are based upon his observation of the Law of Causality (cause and effect), and the Impermanence of all external and internal phenomena.

The First Truth

Suffering, and a liability to suffering, are inherent in all phenomenal life.

Suffering:
- all bodily discomfort or pain;
- all mental discomfort or pain;
- all irritability.

The Second Truth

The Cause of Suffering:
- Ignorance (avijjā);
- Desire (taṇhā) born of ignorance; that is, greed, infatuation with sense objects or ideas, etc.

The Third Truth

The Cessation of Suffering.

The realization that there *is* an escape from suffering, through the discipline followed by all the Buddhas, since this discipline purifies and liberates the mind.

The Fourth Truth

The path that leads away from Suffering.

The Eightfold Noble Path leads the disciple, step by step, beyond the realms of Suffering.

THE EIGHT STEPS OF THE PATH

I. *Right Knowledge*

The Understanding of impermanence in all external phenomena and in all the constituents of personality. Seeing things as they are in reality.[1] Right views, unprejudiced, intelligent, and tolerant.

The disciple will change his ideas as his comprehension of the Dhamma deepens. Living a harmless life, free from all violence (according to the third, the fourth, and the fifth steps), cultivating attentiveness (the seventh step), practising meditation (the eighth step), he will free himself gradually from ignorance.

In this progression, ordinary (lokiya—of the world) ideas will be shed like dead leaves; superior ideas will take their place. *Consciousness will function upon a higher, a transcendental plane* (lokuttara).

II. *Right Aims*

The *immediate* aim is to live the truth that one has ascertained; the distant goal is *liberation* from the limitation of personality and from suffering. Goodwill must be cultivated toward all beings, at all times. One must be determined to get free of attachment to this or that.

[1] Impermanent and conditioned by Suffering.

III. *Right Speech*

Truthful, honest, kindly.

IV. *Right Conduct*

Peaceful, upright, benevolent, peace-bringing.

V. *Right Means of Livelihood*

Any occupation that neither harms nor hinders any living being (that is, causes no suffering to arise).

These steps are based upon the law of non-violence, harmlessness, and the Unity of Life beneath the diversity of all its forms. *Only he who is free from violence is capable of right meditation.*

VI. *Right Effort*

The persevering effort to control thoughts and deeds; to destroy that which is harmful or demeritorious; to cultivate that which is helpful or meritorious; to overcome ignorance and desire; to progress along the Path.

VII. *Right Attention*

Keen observation of life and of all personal thoughts, acts, intentions, and their causes. Observation of the Body and the Mind. Recollection of past experience, awareness of present experience, and thoughtfulness as to the future.

The habit of Attentiveness facilitates analysis and reflection, which are necessary for meditation; it is also productive of right knowledge (the first step).

VIII. *Right Concentration*

Concentration upon one object or idea, to the exclusion of all other ideas.

"Right" concentration is practised to obtain supreme knowledge, not for oneself alone, but for the benefit of all beings.

"If one raises the leg of a table the top of the table will be raised; the man who perfects himself helps all humanity, since all life is interdependent," says Bhikkhu Ananda Kausalyāyana. The power of pure concentrated thought is inestimable.

There are two kinds of concentration:

(1) Preliminary concentration, which leads to (2) Full concentration.

Transcendental states of consciousness (the Jhānas) may be attained in profound meditation. In Jhāna the mind is calm; rapture is experienced.

By living a pure, harmless life, all thoughts, motives, and actions will become less and less selfish; intelligence will be increased; control of the senses and mind-control will be acquired.

Keen observation, investigation, the quest for true

ideas—"these are the requisites for concentration."

| The method | Sīla and Samādhi | The morality of a pure, harmless life Concentration |

lead to

| Wisdom | Paññā and Vipassanā | True Knowledge Insight |

When selfish desire for possessive power and perpetual individuality has been abandoned, a desire for deeper knowledge will arise. Ignorance, greed, and hatred will gradually be eliminated.

Cultivating *Intelligence* and *Compassion* (for one without the other is sterile), the disciple treads the path that all the Buddhas have followed step by step—the Path that leads to liberation.

Beyond Impermanence (phenomenal states) lies "Supreme Existence, which those who are deceived by the delusion of Self call Annihilation." (A. David-Neel.)

Grateful acknowledgment is made to Bhikkhu Sīlācāra for his pamphlet on *Essential Ideas,* which has often been quoted in these pages.

3

CONCENTRATION

Right attention—Sammā-sati
Right Concentration—Sammā-samādhi
The Development of Meditation—Bhāvanā

Right Attention

BUDDHISM considers thought to be of the greatest importance; moreover, if the student wishes to practise meditation, thought must be controlled and directed. With this end in view, it is necessary to cultivate the habit of keen attentiveness.

The disciple should know what motive, what intention, leads him to do this or that. Clearly conscious of his intentions, he will cultivate the habit of observing his body and all external and internal phenomena.

The observation or contemplation of body and mind is explained in the "Meditation upon the Four Fundamentals of Attentiveness" (Chapter 11). The disciple must understand the nature of the constituents as well as the mechanism of the human machine in order to use it properly. This habit of attentive observation will permit him in due time to pursue his intelligent search for the higher knowledge. Right or perfect attention is one of the Seven Factors of Enlightenment.

The disciple must always (at every moment) know what he is doing; he should observe his slightest action and its import. He should watch the "I" or "Self" acting, and the play of phenomena in the universe, where all things are interdependent. Moreover, he must try to observe all this impersonally.

The disciple must understand that this "me," "self," or "I," this personality, is nothing but a group of the five aggregates (Khandhā): form, sensation, perception, discrimination, and consciousness. All these constituents of personality are changing perpetually; therefore there can be no unchanging self, or permanent individuality. This truth must have penetrated the mind before escape from impermanence is possible. The peace of Nibbāna lies beyond grasping personality and can only be attained when the three fires of ignorance, desire, and hate are extinguished.

In the Dīgha Nikāya (22) it is said:

"The disciple is clearly conscious in coming and going; clearly conscious in looking forward and backward; clearly conscious in bending and stretching (any part of his body); clearly conscious in eating, drinking, chewing, tasting; clearly conscious in accomplishing all the natural functions of the body; clearly conscious in walking, standing, sitting, falling asleep, and waking; clearly conscious in speaking and in keeping silent."

It may be said that right attentiveness permits the student to diagnose the ills of life, and that right meditation cures these ills, for meditation tranquillizes and purifies the mind; a sense of physical wellbeing rapidly follows.

Concentration (Samādhi)

There are two degrees of concentration:

1. Preliminary concentration (Upacāra-samādhi);
2. Full concentration (Appanā-samādhi).

Only preliminary concentration should at present be studied. Concentration is obtained when the mind is fixed upon a single subject of thought to the exclusion of every other thought. Concentration is therefore one-pointedness of mind (citt'ekaggatā). This practice develops the intelligence and fortifies the will.

Scientists, artists, and mystics also, often practise concentration unconsciously, but their motives are usually selfish and so in opposition to the right concentration (sammā-samādhi) of the Buddhist.[1]

[1] The Buddhist cultivates concentration knowingly, with the aim of helping others as well as himself.

When concentration upon a subject of meditation has been attained, the field of meditation should be expanded or developed.

The Development of Meditation (Bhāvanā)

Bhāvanā means "that which produces, that which increases." In meditating upon Peace the student increases this thought of Peace until it includes not only himself but also the whole wide world and all beings.

There are two kinds of Bhāvanā:

1. Samādhi-Bhāvanā (Concentration-Development);
2. Vipassanā-Bhāvanā (Insight-Development).

It is the latter which Bhikkhu P. Vajirañāṇa Thero calls "Real Buddhist Meditation," for in such a state of meditation things are seen as they are in Reality.

Insight liberates the aspirant from the three fires of ignorance, desire, and hatred.

It is *liberation*,[1] and not union with any Supreme Being, that the Buddhist seeks. Long before insight-development is possible, consciousness will have been considerably modified and purified by concentration-development.

After Right Attentiveness, Right Concentration, and the Development of Meditation, the Jhānas are

[1] Liberation from greed (lobha), ill will (dosa), and stupidity (moha).

usually studied; but these profound states of meditation (and of ecstasy) cannot be easily understood;
therefore it is proposed to devote an entire chapter
to this subject. Suffice it to say that in scientific mind-
training each thing has its proper place. A tree must
grow its leaves before its fruits appear.

The Jhānas are the fruits (phala) of a pure life and
of pure meditation, but they take time to ripen and
they must be gained. The tree is still a long way off;
the path that leads to it must be trodden step by step,
progressively and methodically, and it must be re-
traced many times.

The student should not seek these states of Jhāna
too soon; they are not even necessary for his progress,
says Bhikkhu Nārada Thero. A pure life and pure
motives of meditation are the essentials. The disciple
should cultivate:

1. Right Attention (Sammā-sati);
2. Right Concentration (Sammā-samādhi);
3. The Development of Meditation (Bhāvanā).

The mind is tranquillized by these practices, and
when the hindrances to meditation have been temporarily eliminated, the disciple will gain a superior
state of consciousness that corresponds to the First
Jhāna.

It is naïve to imagine that Reality can be understood easily; the student must purify and enlighten his mind little by little while living in the phenomenal world, wandering in Saṃsāra.[1] The other shore is far away and the doctrine is a raft that makes it possible for the disciple to cross over beyond.

It may be advisable to examine just what is meant by Right Concentration (Sammā-samādhi)—which is the eighth step upon the Eightfold Noble Path—and also to consider its relationship to the other steps upon that path. This is admirably explained by Bhikkhu Nyānatiloka in the following passages which summarize the various instructions given in this chapter:

RIGHT CONCENTRATION

"Right Concentration (sammā-samādhi), in its widest sense, is that kind of mental concentration which is present in every meritorious state of consciousness (kusala-citta), and is hence accompanied by:

"1. Right-mindedness (sammā-saṅkappa), purified from lust, ill will, and cruelty (second step);

"2. Right effort (sammā-vāyāma), the effort to avoid the arising of evil and demeritorious things that have not yet arisen, and to overcome the evil and

[1] Saṃsāra: perpetual wandering from birth to death and from death to rebirth.

demeritorious things that have already arisen (sixth step);

"3. Right attentiveness (sammā-sati). In all that the disciple is doing he is clearly conscious (1) of his intention; (2) of his advantage; (3) of his duty; (4) of the reality (seventh step).

"The Four Great Efforts (sixth step)—these are the requisites for concentration:

"1. The effort to avoid (demeritorious things);
"2. The effort to overcome (demeritorious things);
"3. The effort to develop (meritorious conditions);
"4. The effort to maintain (meritorious conditions)."

"The practising, developing, and cultivating of these things—this is the Development (Bhāvanā) of concentration."

"Right concentration, or sammā-samādhi, has two degrees of development:

"1. Neighbourhood Concentration (upacāra-samādhi), which approaches the First Jhāna, without, however, attaining it;
"2. Attainment, or Full Concentration (appanā-samādhi), the concentration present in the four Jhānas."

It will be difficult for the student who is a beginner

to concentrate his mind; thoughts foreign to the subject of meditation will dance before him. He must persevere and not become impatient, as this can only weaken his efforts.

When thoughts foreign to the subject of meditation invade his mind, "repetitive thinking" should be practised, as it will prevent the mind from wandering again and again. This has already been mentioned in Chapter 1. It should be understood that repetitive thinking should take the place of consecutive thinking to stabilize the mind and to drive away any intruding thoughts.

Even when full concentration has been attained—"Though at this stage the mind of the aspirant is considerably purified, yet he is not wholly free from giving vent to his passions, for by concentration the evil tendencies of the mind are only *temporarily inhibited*. They may rise to the surface at quite unexpected moments."

"Discipline regulates word and deed; Concentration controls the mind; but it is Insight that enables the disciple to annihilate completely the passions (temporarily inhibited by concentration) (samādhi)." [1]

Progress in Buddhism is logical; reason, intelligence, intuitive knowledge are cultivated in turn. Buddhism does not oppose religion and science, which

[1] Bhikkhu Nārada Thero.

are only different forms of Knowledge.

At any given moment the student has only to do his best; his immediate aim should be to live the truths he has learned through attentive observation of life and right concentration.

4

CHARACTER

It is said that meditation is useful for: the youth who is the man of action; the mature man, who ought to be a man of reflection; and also the man full of years, who should be ripe for meditation.

But certain subjects are suitable for certain characters, while other subjects are quite unsuitable.

If meditation leads to that forgetfulness of "Self" [1] which permits one to look upon life impersonally and to think in terms of unity, it is because the detachment, the serenity, experienced during hours of meditation lasts over and penetrates one's whole life.

The Bhikkhu Parawahera Vajirañāṇa Thero says: "Meditation is an analysis of the relationship existing between mind, matter, and force in its three manifestations: the psychical (nāma), the physiological (rūpa), the psycho-physical (nāma-rūpa). The relationship between the three forms of nāma-rūpa is based on the law of Causality. Every cause is the result of an anterior cause and produces an effect,

[1] Selflessness.

which in its turn will be the cause of an effect. Thus a father creates a søn, the son in turn becomes a father, and so on. The cause is at the same time agent and result."

Everyone does not possess an aptitude for meditation. The "aptitude" is the result of spiritual evolution depending upon the character of the person, and, *up to a certain point,* meditation is not considered absolutely necessary to advancement in the path of liberation.

Buddhist meditation (scientifically pursued) produces a progressive psychical transmutation which profoundly modifies character and develops intelligence.

Calm, and mental happiness, are acquired as one's nature is gradually purified.

The aptitude for meditation must be considered as a privilege that has been earned by the efforts to lead a pure life and to cherish lofty aspirations. The stage of a person's development determines his ability to understand the Dhamma and to practise meditation.

There are

1. Those who are capable of immediately understanding;

2. Those who understand the teaching when it is explained in detail;

3. Those who understand after they have reasoned

it out for themselves and have practised Buddhist morality, which purifies the intelligence as well as the body;

4. Lastly, those who are "like children in the kindergarten," says the Bhikkhu P. Vajirañāṇa Thero.

It is necessary to make a study of the subjects for meditation. The choice of a subject will be determined by the character of each person. This character, as has been said, changes and develops; it depends, at any given moment, upon the corresponding "state of consciousness." [1]

Buddhist psychology has described and defined twenty states of consciousness, whereas only two, the "conscious" and the "subconscious," are recognized in the Occident.

Buddhism has diagnosed the thoughts which afflict humanity as "mental maladies"; in every case they are the result of ignorance. It has also prescribed remedies to cure them.[2]

[1] A comprehensive although abridged study of the states of consciousness, according to the *Abhidhamma Pitaka,* has been written by the late Colonel Dr. Rost, an English Army surgeon and scientist who became a Buddhist in Burma: *The Nature of Consciousness,* by E. R. Rost, Lieut.-Col. I.M.S., O.B.E., etc., published by Williams & Norgate, London, 1930.

The *Abhidhamma Pitaka* ("The Basket of the Transcendental Doctrine") contains the seven books of the Pāli Canon that treat of metaphysics.

[2] 884,000 combinations of mental characteristics are recognized and arranged in forty divisions and six classes.

Characters are divided into six classes, according to the predominant tendency of each:

1. Lustful;
2. Choleric;
3. Ignorant;
4. Incredulous;
5. Credulous;
6. Wise.

The character of a person is determined by and depends upon:

1. The nature of the body;
2. Heredity;
3. Surroundings (environment);
4. The characteristics resulting from personal Kamma (action and result of action).

The habitual repetition of an act or a thought determines the character of a man.

It is said that the Hindus formerly possessed an exact science which enabled them to read character by astrology and also by physiognomy. Each person was considered to be under the influence of one of the four "elements": earth, water, fire, air. The predominating "element" determined the character, and there were meditations that were specially recommended for each type.

There are, however, certain subjects of meditation that can be practised by all students, for they are the antidotes, so to speak, of qualities which are present in almost everyone. Each person should understand the nature of his mind and know what quality or tendency is predominant. He will then be able to correct his undesirable tendencies.

To subdue sudden anger, if one is quick-tempered, one should meditate upon either peace, goodwill, or unselfish love (selfish love is the shadow of hate). Anger and love cannot exist at the same time in the mind. Do not *fight* against an undesirable state of mind, for this only strengthens the thought by concentrating the mind upon it.

Try to *ignore* the undesirable thought, withdraw attention from it, and concentrate upon the opposite quality. If every time that an angry thought arises one calls up thoughts of goodwill, hatred and anger will be driven out.

Above all, try not to discriminate between "oneself" and "others." When there is no distinction, there is no room for hatred. The apparent difference between this and that is superficial; things are not what they seem to be. The appearance and the reality are different; if one can identify oneself in thought with the person who incites anger, angry feelings will cease to exist. This can only be accomplished gradually. Begin by practising tolerance and patience to overcome wrath. Abstain from speaking, endure violent or irritating words for a few moments in silence; in this way one gains self-control.

By such simple means one subdues a quick-tempered disposition. Every other undesirable tendency may be conquered in the same way; that is to say, by concentrating upon the opposite quality and cultivating desirable thoughts. Those whose natures are dominated by passion should concentrate upon peace; they should think of the disadvantages of passion, which inevitably obscures intelligence, and of the advantages of a calm and well-controlled mind.

Those whose natures are cold or insensitive should observe and contemplate the suffering in the world; they should awaken compassion in their hearts and also conjure up sympathy with the good fortune or happiness of others.

The dull-witted need to be stimulated in their efforts to understand; their intelligence will be developed by cultivating attentiveness and by keen observation of external and internal phenomena.[1]

[1] Angry natures should meditate upon Mettā (love) (vide Chapter 10). Passionate or lustful natures should meditate upon Peace (vide Chapter 9). Cold natures should meditate upon Karunā (compassion) and later upon Muditā (sympathetic joy, Chapter 10). The dull-witted or slow of understanding should meditate upon the Four Fundamentals of Attentiveness (Chapter 11) or upon the Body.

Those who are inclined to be incredulous should investigate the ideas that they hold to be true; they should then carefully examine the ideas in which they do not believe. In this way they will prove to themselves the validity of certain truths that hitherto they have not recognized. Those who are inclined to be credulous should not blindly believe in this or that. They should examine all things, not accepting beliefs merely upon faith or tradition; they should find out why they believe this or that to be true and if such a belief is justified by reason. Those who have attained wisdom and understanding of the true nature of phenomena should beware of considering themselves superior; they should remember that they, too, have only acquired their wisdom little by little. All their efforts should be concentrated upon the search for Supreme Knowledge. These are the methods by which one masters and modifies character.

He who meditates is not at all times free from the irruption of undesirable ideas. It is possible that thoughts diametrically opposed to the subject of meditation may spring up suddenly.

While meditating upon Mettā (universal love, or goodwill), lust may be awakened, or a certain ill will may arise. So it is said: "Love has for its near enemy Lust, and for its distant enemy ill will."

Subject	*Near enemy*	*Far enemy*
Love	Lust	Hate
Pity	Aversion	Cruelty

For if love awakens passion, desire is born; this selfish, possessive, blind love is the near enemy. Of such love it is said: "Hatred is the shadow of love." Do not let the mind be caught up in the play of this pair of opposites. Ignore the undesirable idea, concentrate upon benevolent pure love or upon the chosen subject of meditation, and begin again to meditate from the starting-point.

The Buddhist should at all times cultivate unlimited love for all that lives, great or small, strong or weak. By the force of his meditation he creates, he maintains, thoughts of loving goodwill in the universe.

To all those who suffer he should send out thoughts of compassion, he should surround them with boundless compassion. In the same way he should cultivate joy or sympathy for the happiness of others, sympathizing with their good fortune. When he meditates upon Serenity, he should wish that all sentient beings may obtain serenity.

It is not to be forgotten that the Buddhist suffuses *all* living beings, "all that have individuality," with Love, Compassion, Sympathy, and Serenity. These sentiments are not exclusively reserved for human beings, but are to be radiated toward *all that lives*.

These four subjects of meditation (the Four Brahmavihāra explained in Chapter 10) are suitable for nearly every temperament. Certain persons who are supersensitive should not meditate upon Compassion until they can do so without becoming depressed or unduly sentimental.

Character, it has been shown, is modified by thought, as well as by action, which has its origin in thought. To know whether a thought or action is meritorious and will be productive of good, one should ask oneself: "Will this thought or action diminish or increase suffering for me or any other living being?" To a Buddhist this test is infallible.

5

CLASSICAL SUBJECTS OF MEDITATION

It is necessary to give the list of the forty subjects of meditation used by Buddhists of the Southern school, although many of these subjects are not suitable for Westerners.

The classical subjects of meditation are divided into:

1. Meditations with form—Rūpa; and
2. Formless Meditations—Arūpa.[1]

Certain states of consciousness, superior to the usual everyday consciousness, are provoked by certain meditations successfully practised.

It is difficult to try to describe Jhāna (a state of ecstasy that may arise during a profound meditation) to those who are inexperienced in the art of concentration. A chapter is devoted to the choice of suitable subjects for meditation. The choice is necessarily determined by the individual character of each student. He should carefully compare the three chapters on

[1] Where there is no awareness of form (Dr. Rost).

42

Character, Classical Subjects, and Subjects Suitable for Occidental Students.

Kasiṇas—Artifices (or Devices)—were employed to obtain concentration, one-pointedness of mind.

These artifices were used to fix attention and to stabilize the mind. Dr. Rost refers to them as "hypnotic circles."

The Kasiṇas are made of:

1. Earth set in a low frame that has the form of a circle;
2. A bowl of water;
3. An empty globe (air);
4. A circle of light (fire);
5. Coloured stuffs, or pieces of coloured material, blue, yellow Kasiṇa, etc.

A hole in a wall (or in a roof) through which the sky is seen was used for the Space Kasiṇa.

The practiser, concentrating upon the device, after a certain time could see it just as clearly when his eyes were closed as if they were open. Keeping this mental image well in mind, he was then expected to begin his meditation upon a chosen subject. If the Kasiṇa was made of Earth, by enlarging the circle he would think of and see nothing but Earth everywhere—"All is Earth."

It will readily be seen that auto-suggestion played

an important part in this practice, which has been almost abandoned in Ceylon since the death of a famous Guru three hundred years ago.

The Kasinas are said to be still used in Burma.

THE FORTY SUBJECTS OF MEDITATION

(Kammaṭṭhāna)

The seven stations of exercise in calm.

THE TEN KASIṆAS (Artifices or Devices)

1. Earth device	6 Yellow device
2. Water device	7. Red device
3. Air device	8. White device
4. Fire device	9. Light device
5. Blue device	10. Space device

THE TEN ASUBHĀ

The ten stages in the process of decomposition of a corpse.[1]

THE TEN ANUSSATI (RECOLLECTIONS)

1. The Buddha
2. The Doctrine (Dhamma)
3. The Order (Saṅgha)
4. Morality (Sīla)

[1] The Asubhā seem to be unsuitable subjects of meditation for Western students.

5. Giving (Dāna)

6. Higher Beings (Devā)

7. Peace (Upasama)

8. Death (Maraṇa)

9. Attentive observation of the Body (Kāyagatā sati)

10. Attentive observation of Respiration (Ānāpāna sati).

THE FOUR BRAHMAVIHĀRĀ

The Divine States or "The Illimitables": [1]

1. Love (Mettā)

2. Compassion (Karuṇā)

3. Sympathy with the Happiness or the Joy of Others (Muditā)

4. Equanimity, or Serenity (Upekkhā)

THE TWO CONCENTRATIONS

1. The Analysis of the Offensiveness of Material Food (Āhāre paṭikkūlasaññā)

2. The Analysis of the Elements (Catudhātuvavatthānam) [2]

---

[1] These four subjects are suitable and useful for Westerners.
[2] Not the chemical elements, but the "constituents," in the sense of "that which resembles nothing but itself"—e.g., air resembles nothing but air.

The Four Arūpa-Jhānas

1. The Sphere of the Infinity of Space (Ākāsānañcāyatana) [1]

2. The Sphere of the Infinity of Consciousness (Viññānañcāyatana)

3. The Sphere of the Knowledge of No-thingness (Ākiñcaññāyatana)

4. The Sphere of Neither Perception Nor Non-Perception (Nevasaññānāsaññāyatana)

The meditation upon the putrefaction of a corpse should not be allowed to become morbid. The foulness of the corpse should awaken the reflection that dissolution is also continuously taking place in the living body. This meditation is said to destroy lust and to help one to realize the impermanence of personality (the Anattā doctrine), says Dr. Rost.

It is more profitable for modern students to meditate upon the Impermanence of the living body, as this helps to emancipate them from attachment to the "Self." This meditation is included in the meditation upon Respiration, as breathing is an essential function of the body.

---

[1] "Space," Professor Masson-Oursel prefers to translate Akāsa—"*milieu vibratoire.*"

ARŪPA-JHĀNAS

The Formless Meditations

There are four Formless Meditations and four States of Consciousness corresponding to these subjects of meditation (*vide* "Jhānas," Chapter 7).

To practise these meditations all "Awareness of Form" should have disappeared from the mind. "One is no longer conscious of duality or of separateness, there is no desire for sense objects." [1]

It is necessary to have reached the Fourth Jhāna consciousness to meditate upon these subjects (*vide* Chapter 7).

[1] Dr. Barue Dhatt, in *Maha Bodhi Review*, July 1934.

6

SUBJECTS OF MEDITATION SUITABLE

FOR OCCIDENTAL STUDENTS

MEDITATION is a very personal affair. As soon as the student has, through self-observation, understood which characteristics or tendencies are dominant in his nature, it would be advisable to try several subjects of meditation, following the instructions given in Chapter 4. When a suitable subject has been chosen, it should be meditated upon frequently, and during many months. Certain Bhikkhus assert that they have concentrated for years upon the same subject.

A subject that is suitable to the student is one that is agreeable, interesting, and not too difficult for him. Such a subject will calm his mind and permit him to attain concentration easily.

The meditation upon the corpse, which is frequently practised in the Orient, seems unsuitable (in any of its ten forms) for Western students.[1] It would be likely to awaken an æsthetic disgust or to seem

---

[1] The ten Asubhā. *Vide* Chapter 5.

grotesque. It is supposed to bring about detachment from the lure of the flesh. The living body is also to be looked upon as perpetually disintegrating, for certain cells are dying, while others are being born. "This should make one understand Impermanence, and bring about the destruction of lust, but the meditation should not become morbid or morose; it should awaken compassion and comprehension in the student," says Dr. E. R. Rost.

Experience with Western students, practising in meditation classes, seems to prove that the following list of subjects is to be recommended:

Peace, one of the ten recollections (Upasama).

Goodwill, or Love (Mettā).

Pity, or Compassion (Karuṇā).

Joy, or Sympathy with the happiness of others (Muditā).

Equanimity, or Serenity (Upekkhā) (vide Chapter 10).

The Buddha (as intelligence and compassion personified; his virtues; his attainments).

The Dhamma (scientific investigation of the Law, free from the tyranny of creeds or imposed dogmas).

Morality (Sīla). The benefits of non-violence, of cultivating intelligence and compassion, of obtaining control over the body and the mind. Sīla is a discipline freely chosen and self-imposed, which fits one for meditation and leads one to higher states of consciousness.

Giving (Dāna), not charity as usually understood. By freely giving of one's possessions one is liberated from attachment and from the desire for perishable things. In practising Dāna, one purifies oneself, renders service to others, and becomes conscious of the solidarity of all life.

Ānāpāna Sati: the meditation in which special attention is paid to Breathing, as the most important function of the body (*vide* Chapter 13).

These subjects belong to the group of the recollections in which the Peace meditation and the Death meditation are also included.

The Four Fundamentals of Attentiveness:

1. Attentive observation of the Body, paying special attention to Breathing
2. Attentive observation of Sensations
3. Attentive observation of the Mind
4. Attentive observation of Phenomena

Chapter 11 is a study of this important and profitable meditation.

The Three Characteristics of Existence:

1. Anicca—Impermanence—"Transient are all compounded things."

2. Dukkha—Suffering—Phenomenal life is subject to suffering.

3. Anattā—Soullessness—There is no fixed and abiding self (eternal soul) in conditioned or in unconditioned things. (*Vide* Chapter 12.)

The Four Noble Truths:

Studied in the chapter on Essential Ideas (Chapter 2).

In the list of Recollections it will be noticed that the subjects of the Saṅgha and of Death have been omitted.

The Saṅgha is too little understood in the West for a meditation upon this subject to be beneficial. This meditation is for those who have understood the higher paths.

The meditation upon Death, as it is practised in the East, would be likely to produce nothing but depression. This meditation could be very helpful to certain students if they would make it a habit to think of death in the following way:

MEDITATION UPON DEATH

All things are impermanent, all the constituents of the body are constantly changing.

Certain cells are dying, others are coming to be;

death is ever present in the body, bound up with life. Death is nothing but the retreat of consciousness from the body.

Try to be detached from the obsession of clinging to personality.[1] Do not hold on to that which is illusive, impermanent, and unsatisfactory.

Be peaceful; life is so short that it is foolish to waste the days or to be dominated by greed and grasping. It is well to cultivate pure thoughts and higher states of consciousness. Pure thoughts and pure actions are said to ensure rebirth under favourable conditions.

Call to mind the good actions performed in this life and ignore the mistakes; say to oneself:

"There is nothing in death that should frighten; there is nothing in life that should hold one back."

Before falling asleep at night send out loving thoughts to all living beings.

Resolve, when the time comes, to sink peacefully into the sleep of death, free from all regret and from all desire.

Such indeed is the Buddhist attitude toward death and the faring on.

NOTE.—*This meditation may be expanded after the practice-plans have been studied.*

[1] The Oriental seeks liberation from the limits of personality; the Occidental wishes to possess an unchanging immortal Ego.

7

JHĀNAS

RŪPA, ARŪPA, ABHIÑÑĀ, THE FOUR PATHS

BEFORE taking up the subject of Jhāna, it is necessary to recall that Bhāvanā, so often mentioned in the text, has two degrees: [1]

1. Samādhi-Bhāvanā—Concentration-development, and

2. Vipassanā-Bhāvanā—Insight-development.

So far, only concentration-development has been studied and the student has been shown that he may acquire one-pointedness of mind when he is no longer affected by the stimuli of the senses.

The student in Vipassanā-Bhāvanā attains an intuitive vision of Reality, he sees things as they are, he acquires right Knowledge.

When meditation has become wholly subjective, the mind no longer depends upon external objects to attain concentration; it is disciplined and purified. In this condition the four Ecstatic States called the four

[1] *Vide* Foreword, p. ix, "Bhāvanā" (Bhikkhu P. Vajirañāṇa).

Rūpa-Jhānas may perhaps be experienced, for they are the result of successful practice in progressive concentration-development—Samādhi-Bhāvanā.

"The candidate for Nibbāṇa, having reached the Fourth Jhāna, should next turn his mind toward Vipassanā-Bhāvanā (Insight-development)." It is not proposed to study the development of this higher degree of meditation, so far beyond the scope of the ordinary student. Suffice it to say that in due time it may be acquired by those who have successfully practised concentration-development.

The word Jhāna means meditation; it is also applied to certain states of mind that arise as the result of successful meditation. These "Mystical," "Ecstatic" states (or Raptures) have often been misunderstood by Western students of Buddhism.

There is nothing hysterical or abnormal in such states of consciousness. Buddhist meditation is neither emotional nor sentimental; the mind in a state of Jhāna is clear, says Madame A. David-Neel. The Buddhist method of mind-training is scientific; reason and intuitive intelligence are greatly developed by the right practice of meditation, and it is only logical that blissful states of consciousness should result from this training.

The attainment of the trances (Jhānas) is not requisite for the realization of the Four Ultramundane

Paths of Holiness. Insight is attainable only during neighbourhood (preliminary) concentration, says Bhikkhu Nyānatiloka Thero.

RŪPA-JHĀNAS

There are four States of Ecstasy (Jhāna) corresponding to meditations upon subjects with form (Rūpa). They are progressively reached through the successful practice of Samādhi-Bhāvanā (concentration-development).[1]

ARŪPA-JHĀNAS

There are also four States of Ecstasy (Jhāna) corresponding to the four formless (Arūpa) meditations, in meditating upon subjects without form—that is, Space, etc. (*Vide* Chapter 6.)

Each Jhāna will be studied in turn, beginning with the First Rūpa-Jhāna.

The First Jhāna

It has already been said that the hindrances must have been eliminated, and the mind concentrated, before it is possible to attain the First Jhāna.

In the First Jhāna verbal thoughts (vacī sankhārā)

---

[1] It is necessary to have attained the Fourth Rūpa-Jhāna before attempting to reach a state of Arūpa-Jhāna. Five Jhānas are sometimes practised; see p. ix.

are employed; the subject of meditation is analysed and reflected upon. "Sundered from desires and all things evil, exercising cognition and reflection, in the joy and bliss that are born of detachment, he [the aspirant] attains the First High Ecstasy." [1]

The mind will then be impregnated with joy, and a sense of physical and mental well-being—Rapture (or bliss)—is experienced. The First Jhāna is accompanied by five mental attributes which are the opposites of the Hindrances (Dr. E. R. Rost).

Present, in the First Jhāna:

1. Analysis (or cognition)—Vitakka
2. Reflection—Vicāra
3. Joy—Pīti
4. Happiness (well-being)—Sukha
5. Concentration (one-pointedness of mind)—Citt' ekaggatā Samādhi

Absent, in the First Jhāna:

The five hindrances to meditation:

1. Craving
2. Ill will
3. Sloth or torpor
4. Brooding (restless brooding, or any other agitated state of mind)

[1] Bhikkhu Sīlācāra, in his translation of the Sāmaññaphala Sutta.

5. Doubt (or perplexity)

The aspirant is advised not to spend too much time in analysing and reflecting upon the subject of meditation, because his mind may be drawn into the whirlpool of associated ideas, and concentration (one-pointedness) will then be lost.

Only the First Jhāna may be attained by meditating upon such subjects as:

The Cemetery meditation—Asubha-Bhāvanā, and
The Impurities of the body.

It would be better for Westerners to practise one of the meditations upon:

Love—Mettā;
Compassion—Karuṇā;
Sympathy with the joy of others—Muditā.

These subjects of meditation lead to the attainment of the First and also of the Second and the Third Jhānas; they are included in the group of meditations upon the Divine States—Brahmavihārā (Chapter 10).

Each stage of Jhāna is more subtle than the preceding stage.

THE SECOND JHĀNA

In passing from the First to the Second Jhāna, two things are discarded:

1. Analysis, and

2. Reflection.

Three things are *present:*

1. Joy;
2. Happiness;
3. Concentration.

Verbal thinking has been abandoned, there is equal-mindedness. Pure and profound thought persists in a state of joyful bliss.

The Second Jhāna may be attained by meditating upon certain subjects, among which are included: Love, Compassion, Sympathy with the Joy of Others.

THE THIRD JHĀNA

Joy is absent; it will have been abandoned, for it is impermanent and therefore not the Goal.

Two things are *present:*

1. Happiness;
2. Concentration.

The mind is intensely concentrated, blissful, and clearly conscious.

The Third Jhāna may be attained by meditating upon:

Love;

Compassion;

Sympathy with the Happiness of Others.

THE FOURTH JHĀNA

In each Jhāna the mind becomes progressively more concentrated; consciousness becomes more and more subtle. In the Fourth Jhāna the sensation of happiness has disappeared. There is no consciousness of pleasure or of pain. Only serenity and one-pointedness of mind exist. Thought is absolutely purified, serene, and concentrated.

Present:

Equanimity or Serenity (indifference to pleasure and pain)

The Fourth Jhāna may be attained by meditating upon:

Attentive observation of breathing (Ānāpāna Sati), or

Serenity (Upekkhā) (which is the fourth subject in the group of the "Divine States").

The Buddhist does not practise Jhāna because of the happiness experienced in such a state; he aims at spiritual progress. In Jhāna he acquires detachment and understanding of the teaching (Dhamma).

In the Saṃyutta Nikāya 21, it is said: "Develop concentration, for he who is concentrated understands things as they are in reality. Which things?

"1. Form—Rūpa;

"2. Sensation—Vedanā;

"3. Perception—Saññā;

"4. Mental formations (activities)[1]—Saṅkhārā;

"5. Consciousness—Viññāṇa.

"These are the five Khandhā, or attributes of being, which may be understood through meditation." These aggregates compose personality.

ARŪPA-JHĀNA

As has been stated, there are four states of consciousness corresponding to the four meditations upon formless subjects. These states of ecstasy arise during a meditation upon:

1. Space as infinite;
2. Consciousness as infinite;
3. The Knowledge of No-thingness; [2]
4. The plane where there is neither Perception nor yet Non-Perception.

Equanimity and one-pointedness of mind are the only mental factors present in meditations without form.[3]

---

[1] "The aggregates of those states of mind which produce meritorious or demeritorious actions." *Vide* Chapter 13, "Ānāpāna Sati," for the progressive liberation from "this and that" state of mind. The Second Tetrad—VII Citta.

[2] "No-thingness," where there is no idea or object present in the mind.

[3] Dr. E. R. Rost: *The Nature of Consciousness.*

Certain Rūpa meditations precede and prepare one for the Arūpa meditations and their corresponding states of mind.

A meditation upon Compassion prepares one to meditate upon Space, etc.

No one should attempt to meditate upon formless subjects until he has mastered the practice of concentration and has attained success in meditating upon subjects with form (either ideas or objects).

SPACE (ĀKĀSA)

To explain the procedure employed in meditating upon a formless subject, the Space meditation is given here. But (as has been said) the student must not practise Arūpa-Jhāna until an abstract meditation is not too difficult for him. Moreover, it is stated that the four Rūpa-Jhānas must have been reached before beginning an Arūpa meditation.

The Space meditation should be preceded by a meditation upon Compassion (Chapter 10), for "pity frees the heart from egoism." In the Arūpa-Jhānas no egoism, no sense of duality (self and others), is present.

The student, seated or lying upon his back (in the open air), should look at the sky and notice the space between the clouds; he should think:

Space is boundless, infinite.

Space is everywhere.

Space is within everything.

He should then think of the space between the stars, of the space between the cells of the body. He should fill his mind with the idea of Space and think of nothing else.

After a certain lapse of time let him imagine that the clouds have disappeared, the trees have sunk into the ground, the earth has disappeared.

He should identify himself with Space and be conscious only of Space.

The Space meditation seems to be the only one of the formless meditations that is suitable for certain advanced students in the Occident. But if other formless meditations should be attempted, a preliminary meditation always should be practised.

To prepare for meditating upon Consciousness as Infinite, the student should begin by practising a meditation upon Sympathy with the Joy of Others.

The Third and Fourth Arūpa-Jhānas

The knowledge of No-thingness.

The plane of Neither Perception Nor yet of Non-Perception cannot be attained under the usual conditions of life in the Occident.

The transition from one state of Rūpa-Jhāna to

the next higher state is determined by "seeing the imperfection of the lower, as compared to the higher state." Since joy and bliss are impermanent, they are considered imperfect, and the aspirant seeks a state where he will be liberated definitely from "this and that"—that is, from all limiting ideas and all sense of duality.

It is not "Ecstasy" (Jhāna) but "Insight" (Vipassanā) that the Buddhist should incessantly seek, and this may be obtained in neighbourhood concentration.[1]

The four Rūpa-Jhānas (the meditations with form) and the four Arūpa-Jhānas (the formless meditations) belong to the cosmic plane (lokiya).[2] They gladden and calm the mind; this is useful as it precedes insight (Vipassanā), but they cannot lead (by themselves alone) to the Four Paths of the ultramundane, the supernormal (lokuttara). That is to say, they cannot liberate us *definitely* from all demeritorious and harmful tendencies.

The Five Jhānas

Five Jhānas are sometimes practised when one

[1] Upacāra—neighbourhood or preliminary concentration; Appanā—full concentration; i.e., that which is present in the Jhānas.
[2] Lokiya is the plane upon which the worldly or everyday consciousness functions. Lokuttara is a higher plane of consciousness reached by the "Noble Disciples."

wishes to pass from a meditation with form to a meditation without form.

In that case the First Jhāna is divided into two stages, by retaining sustained application of mind (reflection) in the Second Jhāna (where it is usually absent), and dropping it in the Third Jhāna.

In this division, therefore:

I. The First Jhāna has *present:*
    1. Analysis (Vitakka);
    2. Reflection (i.e., verbal thinking—Vicāra);
    3. Joy (Pīti);
    4. Happiness, or Bliss (Sukha);
    5. Concentration (Ekaggatā).

II. The Second Jhāna.

Remember that in passing to the Second Jhāna, *only* Analysis is dropped. There will therefore be *present:*

    1. Reflection;
    2. Joy;
    3. Happiness;
    4. Concentration.

III. The Third Jhāna will have *present:*

    1. Joy;
    2. Happiness;

3. Concentration.

IV. The Fourth Jhāna will have *present:*

1. Happiness;
2. Concentration.

V. The Fifth Jhāna will have *present:*

1. Concentration.

The five Jhānas are practised when one is seeking to acquire "supernormal intellection"—Abhiññā.

ABHIÑÑĀ

Supernormal Intellection

It is said that the superior states of consciousness, which are acquired in the Jhānas, may lead to certain supernormal powers or faculties.[1]

It is to obtain these powers that the aspirant practises five, instead of the usual four, Jhānas.

These psychic powers are:

1. Supernormal accomplishments,
2. Clairvoyance,
3. Clairaudience,

[1] Iddhis—psychic powers; Abhiññā—supernormal intellection (Dr. E. R. Rost). T. W. Rhys Davids gives "Potencies" for Abhiññā. Iddhis and Abhiññā are often used to mean the same thing.

4. Memory of previous births,

5. Power to read the past history of other beings.

The order is sometimes differently given.

The Buddhist speaks of rebirth and not of reincarnation, as the latter implies an immortal (or unchanging) self. But there is said to be *continuity of consciousness* from life to life; therefore it is deemed possible to remember past lives.

The aspirant begins by remembering his thoughts and deeds from hour to hour; then from day to day, month to month, year to year, etc., until he arrives at the moment of birth. After a certain amount of practice, he will be able to remember his death, and later on he will call to mind his previous existence and then other existences.

This practice should enable the aspirant to understand the thoughts and deeds (in the past) which have conditioned his present existence; therefore it should enable him to eliminate his undesirable tendencies. In the same way it will permit him to observe and understand the Kamma (action and result of action) of other beings.

These exercises, which force memory, are not to be recommended; they are only mentioned here as "by-products" of meditation.

Bhikkhu Sīlācāra is thoroughly against this practice; he writes: "When one has gone far upon the

Path, this 'Memory' comes as an unfailing by-product of that advance. In my opinion it should come naturally, not unnaturally."

The Four Paths

There are ten fetters, which bind all Beings to the wheel of existence.

The Fetters (Saññojana)

1. The illusion of self;
2. Scepticism;
3. Attachment to Rites and Ceremonies (considering them efficacious in obtaining liberation);
4. Sensual lust;
5. Ill will;
6. Craving for life in the world of Pure Form;
7. Craving for the Formless World;
8. Pride;
9. Agitation;
10. Ignorance.

The First Path

A "Stream-Winner" (Sotāpanna), one who has entered the stream leading to Nibbāna, is upon the First Path, which he has attained by getting rid of the first three fetters. He will be reborn no more than seven times.

The Second Path

A "Once-Returner" (Sakadāgāmin) has overcome the fourth and fifth fetters, in their grosser form. He will return to this sphere only once more.

The Third Path

The "Non-Returner" (Anāgāmin) is wholly freed from the first five fetters which bind to rebirth in Kāma-loka (world of sense). When he dies he will reach the goal, while living in the sphere of Pure Form.

The Fourth Path

The "Perfect" or "Holy One" (Arahat) is free from all the ten fetters.

All those upon the Holy Paths have ultramundane right understanding (lokuttara sammā ditthi), which is not of the world, in contradistinction to the ordinary mundane right understanding (lokiya sammā ditthi). In other words, there is an ordinary and a higher (transcendental) understanding of the Noble Eightfold Path.

RÉSUMÉ

It has been shown that concentration leads to mind-control and that meditation gradually purifies the whole nature of man. Moreover, intelligence is increased by this practice. When a higher state of consciousness has been reached, the student soon will find that his ideas and his outlook upon life have changed.

As his ignorance decreases he will rid himself gradually of the impediments to progress upon the Noble Eightfold Path. Through Morality (Sīla) and Concentration (Samādhi) he will arrive at Wisdom (Paññā).

It has been said that his outlook upon life will depend at any given moment upon the stage of his spiritual evolution. He has only to do his best and to follow his *own* light, for this light will become stronger and clearer as veil after veil of ignorance disappears.

This statement may be applied, not only to the disciple who is attempting to follow the first steps upon the Path, but also to those "noble disciples" who have gained Path consciousness. "Be ye lamps unto yourselves."

The student should re-read these chapters after he has acquired a certain skill in practising the various meditations in Part II.

PART II

PRACTICE

8

PREPARATION—POSTURE—
RESPIRATION

HE WHO desires seriously to practise meditation should consider these words of Bhikkhu Nārada Thero: "For the aspirant the first stage on the path is Sīla (moral discipline). Without killing or causing the slightest harm to any living being, he should be kind and compassionate toward all, even toward the smallest creature that grovels at his feet. Abstaining from thieving, either openly or secretly, he should be straight and honest in all his transactions. Abstaining from wrong indulgence in physical passions, he should be pure and chaste. Abstaining from false speech, he should be sincere. Avoiding intoxicants and pernicious drugs, he should be sober and diligent. These five precepts should be strictly observed, for transgression of them is likely to create new difficulties and to raise up obstacles which are almost insurmountable."

The student having thoroughly realized the importance of Sīla should now consider the first general rules for successful meditation.

Never tire the mind or the body.

Too much tension and forced application only make meditation more difficult.

PREPARATION

Time

One should not begin meditation too soon after eating.[1] The process of digestion should have run its course; this is likely to take two or three hours.

Cleanliness

The body and the clothing should be scrupulously clean.

Place

One should retire to a quiet place, or a room where one will not be disturbed by any intruders or noises.

If possible it is best to set aside a room, however small, for meditation. This is the custom in many houses in Ceylon, even among the unwealthy. A secluded spot beneath a tree, when in the country, is a favourite and favourable place for meditation. Peace

[1] It is better not to eat heavy food, alcohol is entirely forbidden by the Southern school, and it is obviously illogical for a Buddhist to be carnivorous; a difference of opinion exists upon this subject, but all seem to agree that he who is training for meditation should abstain from meat.

and solitude are necessary. For certain meditations absolute silence is essential.

POSTURE

A comfortable position should be chosen; the body should be at ease, so that no strain or fatigue is felt, and one is able to remain in the same position for a certain length of time without moving.

The classic position in vogue in the Orient is unsuitable for Occidentals, as the crossing and flattening of the legs is likely to be difficult.

This position slows down the circulation in the lower half of the body so that more blood flows toward the upper half, and the activity of the brain is increased by the blood-supply. The unsupple Occidental will more likely be at ease in a comfortable chair; he must keep the spinal column straight and the head erect (so that they form a straight line).

The feet should be crossed, the right ankle resting upon the left ankle, the right hand (with the palm open) should rest upon the left hand. The field of vision should be limited, therefore the eyes should be half-closed, or closed—if one can do so without becoming drowsy. Imagine that thought is concentrated at a definite spot just between the eyebrows.

Beginners should take this position and hold it for five or ten minutes daily to train the body so that one will not have to pay attention to it when one begins meditation.

It will be found helpful to practise each day at the same hour and in the same place. The student should be seated facing east.

Next in order come the breathing-exercises which help the student to fix his attention and to concentrate.

RESPIRATION

The breathing-exercises of Hatha Yoga are often confused by the public with Buddhist practices; they are, however, distinctly different. Purification, respiration, and rhythmic respiration are the only Yogic exercises practised by certain Southern Buddhists and not considered dangerous.

To quote Bhikkhu P. Vajirañāṇa Thero: "The Yogic and Buddhist breathing-exercises practised in meditation are different but go together."

Yoga is undoubtedly a science which permits one to obtain an unusual control of body and mind. Buddhists consider many Yogic practices to be exaggerated, incompatible with the middle path which avoids extremes.

The true Buddhist method of practising breathing-exercises is fully explained in the chapter on Ānāpāna Sati. Hindu Yoga existed before the advent of the Buddha Gotama; his early masters, Āḷāra and Uddaka, were Yogins; he rejected their extreme practices as not leading to liberation. But Yoga was not systematized until the time of Patanjali and "seems to have come under the influence of Buddhism," according to the well-known Sanskrit scholar Bhikkhu Rahula Sankrityāyana. The word Yoga, when employed by a Hindu, means union with Brahma (the Supreme Being), while to a Buddhist Yoga means "a method of discipline helpful for obtaining Nibbāṇa." [1] Breathing-exercises are, in both Yoga and Buddhism, a part of preliminary training for meditation.

According to the Hindus, the body as it takes in air also absorbs Prāna (vital energy) which is latent in the atmosphere.

YOGIC BREATHING

I. The Purifying Breath

To purify the respiratory system, close the right nostril, compressing it with the forefinger; at the same time breathe in through the left nostril. Hold the air for a few seconds. Blow out the air through the right nostril; then compress the left nostril while drawing in the air through the right nostril and

[1] Many other Hindu words are employed in Buddhism in a different sense: Brahma in Buddhism means a superior (or higher) state; Attā (immortal soul to a Hindu) in Buddhism means personality or individuality, which, since it is impermanent, cannot be considered "immortal."

holding it for a few seconds. Repeat this practice, alternately compressing and freeing the nostrils, several times. The whole respiratory system will be cleansed of impure air.

Claude Bragdon (in his *Introduction to Yoga*) advises inhaling during four seconds, holding the air for sixteen seconds, exhaling gently and regularly during eight seconds. He advises repeating this exercise ten times before beginning a meditation. This retention of the breath during sixteen seconds may be disadvantageous for beginners. It is perhaps more prudent to:

Inhale while counting eight;

Hold the breath while counting four (slowly);

Exhale while counting eight;

Stop breathing; let the lungs remain empty while counting four.

II. Rhythmical Breathing

Rhythmical breathing may be practised at any time, while one is resting or when one is taking a walk. The counts should be based upon or correspond to the heart-beats of the person practising—that is to say, neither faster nor slower than the normal pulsation of one's heart.

Empty the lungs of air while counting six gently and regularly;

Stop breathing (arrest the breath) while counting three;

Inhale, filling the lungs with air while counting six;

Retain the air while counting three.

This includes lower, middle, and higher breathing. Repeat this exercise, breathing regularly, rhythmically, at least ten times.

The counts may be increased after a certain amount of experience has been acquired. The time counted during the retention of the breath and during the arrested breathing should (at any rate for beginners) be one-half as long as the time of exhaling and inhaling. If the breath is held too long, disagreeable sensations such as dizziness will be experienced. If a Buddhist uses these exercises he avoids exaggerating the suspended breaths. Rhythmic breathing should purify the body, calm the mind, and fortify the nervous system. It should never produce fatigue. These two exercises are part of Prānāyāma as practised in various systems of Hindu Yoga.

III. Buddhist Breathing

Certain authorities, such as Dr. Cassius Pereira, of Ceylon, see no necessity for employing Yogic breathing: "Normal breathing should not at any time be forced or suspended. One should only attentively observe the respiration and note the variations until concentration of mind is attained." (*Vide* Chapter 13, C. Pereira.)

COUNTING

Counting is employed as a means of fixing attention; it helps one to obtain preliminary concentration. There are of course many ways of counting. Certain Bhikkhus, and two masters of the Zen sect who were consulted, advise beginners to count mentally up to fifty or to one hundred while thinking of nothing but the counts. He who is able to count one hundred (in ten series of ten) without any distraction has learned to concentrate. It is still better if one can count up to three hundred uninterrupted by stray thoughts.

"The simplest method is to be *keenly interested*, so that the counting does not become mechanical or fatiguing, and then to take up the subject of the meditation. The subject should have been chosen beforehand and should thoroughly interest the student. Let him be precise, prepare the subject of meditation, and examine it. Let him take time and not struggle; mental resistance will gradually diminish," says Dr. Kirby, Abbot of a Zen monastery. "However diligent one may be, initial difficulties cannot be avoided. Thoughts foreign to the meditation will intrude. The beginner should not be discouraged; repeated practice and sustained resolution will always bring about results. Sometimes more rapidly than expected."

These indications seem to answer the questions that are usually asked by beginners. To avoid any mistake, definite instructions as to position, breathing, repetition of the subject,[1] the development of meditation (Bhāvanā), etc., are given in the practice-plans explained in the following chapters.

THE HINDRANCES

When the "physical approach" to meditation has been regulated (position, breathing, etc.), the "mental approach" must be prepared. One must get rid of the "hindrances to meditation" to purify the mind and permit it to be calm and clear. There are five mental states (or modes of thought) that hinder, or prevent, successful meditation:

1. Craving;
2. Ill will;
3. Sloth (and torpor);
4. Restless brooding (agitated states of mind);
5. Doubt (or perplexity).

To rout out and banish any one of these mental states, Bhikkhu Sīlācāra's advice is to concentrate upon a thought directly contrary to it rather than to fight

[1] "Repetitive thinking."

against it. If a thought of ill will arises, think of benevolence.

When the body and the mind have been properly prepared,[1] according to the instructions given in this chapter, the student may begin to practise concentration.

Let him remember:

1. *Not to tire the body or the mind.*

2. *To choose a subject of meditation that interests him.*

3. *To repeat the subject, if the mind wanders;* that is, if meditating Peace, to repeat: "Peace, Peace," etc.

4. *To persevere.*

[1] Posture, respiration, mind-purification having been established.

9

MEDITATION UPON PEACE

UPASAMA-BHĀVANĀ

IN CHOOSING a subject of meditation suitable for those students who live under modern conditions in the Western world, the Peace meditation will prove the most beneficial. Peace of mind is a necessity for inner life and spiritual growth.

The approach to meditation is not easy for a beginner, but the method presented here can easily be understood and applied without difficulty by any student who sincerely desires to practise, provided he has reached a stage of spiritual evolution which renders him "apt or fit for meditation." Moreover, by a cunningly contrived combination of breathing-exercises (following purely Buddhist traditions) and moments of silent thought, body and mind attain that calm which precedes and permits concentration.

The student develops the meditation progressively and, for a few seconds (at first), he will presently be able to efface *verbal thinking*, to experience the Silence of Pure Thought beyond words.

Instruction in the use of this method was given me by a hermit, a Canadian, the Samaṇa Mahinda, meditating in the forests of Ceylon. He in turn had received the teaching from the Ven. Siliva, who had especially elaborated a method suitable for Occidentals.[1]

I have added an abridged practice-plan useful for class meditation, advising each student to have it constantly before his eyes while training, and to memorize it as soon as possible.

The Threefold Refuges (Ti Saraṇa) of all who take refuge in the Buddha, in his Teaching, and in the Order are recited in Ceylon at the beginning of every meditation. This ancient and useful custom will be meaningless unless one understands the reverence and gratitude due to the Compassion-Intelligence of the Enlightened One. Those who desire to omit it may begin with the breathing-exercises.

It will be found profitable for all students to practise the Peace meditation during their various stages of progress. It may well serve as the only subject for a long time, and later it will be useful as a preliminary exercise before meditating upon some other subject.

When the student has decided to live a life whose ideal (at least) is purity, when he has determined to

[1] I was permitted to practise this meditation in classes composed of adults and children.

avoid inflicting suffering (as far as lies in his power) upon any sentient being, if he has understood the advantages of meditation and has resolved to practise strenuously, he is then properly prepared to study the method.

The subject chosen is Peace.

> Perfect cleanliness,
> Comfortable clean clothing,
> A quiet place, and
> A comfortable position are necessary preliminaries.

METHOD AND INSTRUCTIONS OF THE VEN. MAHINDA

Position

According to the Ven. Mahinda, a comfortable position is insisted upon because it permits one to obtain complete relaxation, to be quiet, and to avoid moving during a certain length of time. It is essential to keep the spinal column straight and the head erect.

The student should learn to focus his attention at a point between the eyes; let him imagine that his thought is concentrated in his forehead at a point just between the eyebrows.

The breath should be inhaled and exhaled through the nostrils. He should now *attentively* follow the course of the breath as he breathes in and out.

The beginner may experience a certain difficulty

in observing these instructions, but this will soon be overcome.

Success in meditation depends upon one's own effort; through sincerity and perseverance the student is sure of obtaining good results. Moreover, this method has been so contrived that it permits anyone to meditate without danger; it is based upon "mindfulness as to respiration" as a means for acquiring concentration and follows purely Buddhist traditions.

Beginners will find that it is easier for several people to practise together with a leader, to control the breathing-exercises and to see that the instructions are both well understood and strictly observed.

As soon as the student is sufficiently trained he should usually practise alone.

Begin by reciting the Three Refuges.

Ti Saraṇa

To the Buddha for Refuge I go.
To the Dhamma for Refuge I go.
To the Saṅgha for Refuge I go.

For the second time: "To the Buddha," etc.
For the third time: "To the Buddha," etc.

With eyes half-closed and looking toward the tip of the nose (to limit the field of vision) practise the breathing-exercises, saying to oneself:

"A long breath I breathe in." ⎫
"A long breath I breathe out." ⎬ 10 times
                 ⎭

Inhale and exhale slowly, taking long, deep breaths.[1]
Then breathe quickly and superficially, saying:

"A short breath I breathe in." ⎫
"A short breath I breathe out." ⎬ 10 times
                  ⎭

Let your thought follow attentively the breath as you inhale and exhale; concentrate upon it. Notice and feel the contact of the air with the nostrils. Breathe gently—easily—do not force or produce contractions.

Begin with ten respirations, increasing by one count each week.[2]

After the long and short breaths, return to normal breathing during thirty counts (inhaling and exhaling). Let the breathing regulate itself normally, observing it attentively.

One is now prepared to meditate on the subject chosen—Peace.

A

Say to yourself:
I am Peace.

[1] Usually one should begin by outbreathing to get rid of impurities; here one may presume that this has been done already.
[2] Never go too far.

Surrounded by Peace.
I dwell safely in Peace.
Peace is above, beneath, within me.
Such Peace is mine—
And all is well.

Think Peace

During fifteen seconds think of the meaning of
Peace, then try to understand its significance, to feel
an impression of absolute Peace.

Take your time, think attentively, without haste,
and clearly, and understand that you are consciously
directing mind by mind (the conscious mind by the
subconscious).

B

Stop Thinking

Eliminate verbal thinking. For fifteen seconds silence your thoughts. "Blank" your mind.

Observe your breathing only. Be concentrated, be
still, be silent mentally so that the *idea,* the significance, the sensation of Peace may sink into you, be
absorbed, and work its way.

During this time you should be aware of nothing
else than breathing. Direct mind by mind.

C

Create a mental picture

During fifteen seconds make a mental picture of yourself. See yourself attentively living, meaning, feeling Peace and its significance in thought, word, and deed.

Let the mental image be definite and clear, visualizing yourself in your home, in the street, at your usual occupations, at work, peaceful, and full of Peace. Remember that in so doing you are directing the conscious or external mind by the subconscious or corporeal mind.

Return through the stages B and A, the short and long breathing-exercises, and the recital of the.Three Refuges.

This method is bound to bring results if it is practised sincerely and regularly. The breathing-exercises help one to obtain concentration and prepare for meditation upon the Dhamma (the Law, the Teaching).

Before beginning the meditation, repeat the subject several times: Peace . . . Peace . . . Peace . . . etc.

EXTRA INSTRUCTIONS

Respiration

Increase the long and short breaths by one count each week, having practised daily.

Increase the normal breathing by ten counts each week.

Practise this method every day at the same hour, and, if possible, twice a day, in the morning and late in the evening.

Such practice can lead to a state of First Jhāna, a state of ecstatic meditation (see Chapter 7).

Silent Thinking

Increase the stage of silent thinking by one count each week.

One should try to distinguish the difference between verbal thinking and silent thought.

Through this training one should eventually arrive at the state of Second Jhāna.

The Mental Picture

Increase the time of holding in your mind a mental picture of yourself by one second every week.

During the day you should try to recall the mental image of yourself acting Peace. You should try to conform your daily living to this vision of yourself as seen while meditating Peace, or other subjects such as Joy, Serenity, etc.

This should in due time help you to reach higher states of consciousness.

The more clearly you succeed in visualizing this mental picture, and the longer you hold it in mind, the easier will it be for you to obtain one-pointedness of mind.

This method will permit you to draw up plans for meditations on other suitable subjects and to practise meditation when and where you will. It should therefore be studied carefully in detail and well understood; a sincere effort is all that is needed to obtain good results.

Advice to Beginners

During the day cultivate the habit of thinking about the subject of your meditation.

Visualize yourself practising attentively: Goodwill, Joy, Wisdom, Silence, etc.

As soon as you have acquired sufficient training in the Peace formula, you should continue to develop the meditation, enlarging your horizon as follows:

Outside of meditation hours watch yourself in your home, imagine that you are surrounded by Peace, living in Peace, bathing in Peace, your whole being absolutely peaceful and radiating Peace toward all sentient beings that live and breathe. Keep this picture of yourself filled with Peace well fixed in your mind. Then imagine that all persons, all the inmates of the house, are surrounded by Peace, living in Peace, bathed in Peace.

Visualize them as being absolutely peaceful, radiating Peace in thought, word, and deed toward all living beings. Imagine that every room in the house is surrounded by Peace, steeped in Peace, and radiating Peace. Hold this picture well in mind.

Imagine that you are leaving the house; see your home surrounded by Peace; see it and its inmates established in perfect Peace.

Imagine that you are walking down the street, and that each person who passes is surrounded by Peace, living in Peace, steeped in Peace, radiating Peace in thought, word, and deed toward all sentient beings. This mental picture should be fixed in your mind so that you can recall it at any moment.

Fancy that you continue your walk. Observe the different people engaged in diverse occupations; imagine that they are surrounded by Peace, that Peace enters and passes through them and is radiated through all their thoughts, words, and deeds toward all sentient beings.

Imagine yourself in a crowd that is surrounded by Peace, living in Peace, flooded with Peace; see yourself wrapped in Peace, feeling absolutely peaceful, dispensing Peace in every thought, word, and deed toward all that lives and breathes. You must remember this mental picture.

Observe the changing crowd and the different faces attentively. See each one of them surrounded by Peace, Peace flowing over them and radiating through each thought, word, and deed toward all living beings.

You should imagine, feel, and be conscious of nothing but Peace, that Peace for which each man yearns and aspires.

You should see Peace everywhere, in everything, and in all living and sentient beings. See Peace always present somewhere in the universe. No one is responsible for the sayings or doings of others; all that you should feel and see is the Peace within each heart, whether one is conscious of it or not.

Knowing, feeling, and acknowledging that Peace is deeply hidden in them, you are thereby freed from the thoughts, words, and deeds of people around you, and you will see and feel nothing but Peace. You are the master of your thoughts, you are able to choose (or reject) what you will feel or will not feel. Your feelings are directed by your thoughts.

Through this training you will have cultivated the habit of Right Attentiveness and Right Concentration on the subject of meditation, Peace.

A plan for meditation classes summarizing the instructions of the Ven. Mahinda follows. It should be carefully studied and memorized as soon as possible. It may be used as a guide for meditation upon other subjects and will prevent the beginner from losing the thread in the labyrinth of vagrant thoughts, thus permitting him to obtain access to concentration.

PRACTICE-PLAN

PEACE MEDITATION

Ti Saraṇa (The Threefold Refuge)

Buddhaṁ saraṇaṁ gacchāmi,
Dhammaṁ saraṇaṁ gacchāmi,
Saṅghaṁ saraṇaṁ gacchāmi,

Dutiyampi Buddhaṁ saraṇaṁ gacchāmi,
Dutiyampi Dhammaṁ saraṇaṁ gacchāmi,
Dutiyampi Saṅghaṁ saraṇaṁ gacchāmi,

Tatiyampi Buddhaṁ saraṇaṁ gacchāmi,
Tatiyampi Dhammaṁ saraṇaṁ gacchāmi,
Tatiyampi Saṅghaṁ saraṇaṁ gacchāmi.

Ti Saraṇa (The Threefold Refuge)

(TRANSLATION)

To the Buddha for refuge I go,
To the Dhamma for refuge I go,

To the Sangha for refuge I go.

For the second time: To the Buddha . . . etc.

For the third time: To the Buddha . . . etc.

Choose a comfortable posture.

Relax the body and the mind.

Half close the eyes—gazing toward the tip of the nose.

Observe the breathing. Empty the lungs of impure air before beginning.

Think:

"A long breath I breathe in."

  1   2   3   4   5   10 times

"A long breath I breathe out."

  1   2   3   4   5

Think:

"A short breath I breathe in."

  1 2 3 4 5   10 times

"A short breath I breathe out."

  1 2 3 4 5

Normal breathing—   For 30 seconds.

Stop thinking—blank the mind.   For 15 seconds.

Be silent, be still.

Observe the breathing as you inhale and exhale.

As the breath strikes against the nostrils, do not think about it, only be *aware* that breathing is going on.

Think Peace: [1]

I am Peace,
Surrounded by Peace,
I dwell safely in Peace,
Peace is above, beneath, within me,
Such Peace is mine,
And all is well.

Peace to all beings.
Peace between all beings.
Peace from all beings.

(Imagine all beings sending you only peaceful thoughts.)

I am filled with Peace,
I am saturated with Peace,
I am absorbed in Peace.

Stop thinking—blank the mind. For 15 seconds.

Observe the breathing.

Be silent, be still. Look within.

[1] Hold each thought for 10 or 15 counts mentally. Let the thought sink in.

Make a mental picture of yourself. For 15 seconds.

See yourself at home—

Acting Peace,
Thinking Peace,
Meaning Peace.

Observe yourself
as though you were
another person.

Abroad—on the street, at work, in the shops, etc.,
always

Acting Peace,
Thinking Peace,
Meaning Peace.[1]

Stop thinking—blank the mind.
Observe your breathing.   For 15 seconds.

RETURN

Make a mental picture of yourself. For 15 seconds.
See yourself:

Abroad—

Acting Peace,
Thinking Peace,
Meaning Peace.

[1] At this point a meditation on another subject may be chosen or
you may begin to return through B and A.

Blank the mind for 15 seconds; watch your respiration. Make a
mental picture (as described above). Blank the mind, and observe
the breathing. Other subjects: Mettā—love. Paññā—Wisdom. Karuṇā
—Pity. Pīti—Joy.

At home—

> Acting Peace,
> Thinking Peace,
> Meaning Peace.

Stop thinking—blank the mind. For 15 seconds.
Observe your breathing.

Think Peace. (15 seconds between each phrase.)

> I am filled with Peace,
> I am saturated with Peace,
> I am absorbed in Peace.

> Peace to all beings,
> Peace between all beings,
> Peace from-all beings.

> I am Peace,
> Surrounded by Peace,
> I dwell safely in Peace,
> Peace is above,
>> beneath,
>> within me.
> Such Peace is mine,
> And all is well.

Normal Breathing.   For 30 seconds.

A short breath I breathe in.

1 2 3 4 5

A short breath I breathe out.

1 2 3 4 5

10 times

A long breath I breathe in.

1   2   , 3   4   5   ⎫
                                       ⎬ 10 times
A long breath I breathe out.   ⎭

1   2   3   4   5

Open the eyes.

Ti Saraṇa

Advanced students of meditation will have noticed that beginners who practise this method, especially designed for Westerners, are taught (almost imperceptibly) the essentials of Buddhist meditation.

In A: preliminary concentration on breath (as a function of the body necessary to maintain life).

In B: to silence for a few seconds verbal thinking, "the monkey mind," to contact Pure Thought.

In C: to create an image which serves as a device (kasiṇa) to prevent the mind from wandering. Moreover, looking upon oneself as an actor playing a part, one will learn, little by little, to observe oneself impersonally as in the meditation on the Four Fundamentals of Attentiveness.

G. C. L.

10

MEDITATION UPON
THE FOUR DIVINE STATES

THE meditations on the Four Divine States or Superior States (Brahmavihārā), sometimes called Infinite Sentiments (Appamaññā), are important and thoroughly suitable for Western students.[1]

1. Mettā means Love in the sense of benevolence or loving-kindness.

2. Karuṇā is compassion, or pity for all suffering.

3. Muditā is joyous sympathy with the happiness of other beings.

4. Upekkhā is equal-mindedness—that is, a state of Serenity, or indifference to joy or sorrow.

I

METTĀ

Several formulas are given for the Love meditation.

---

[1] In the Buddhist Scriptures these subjects of meditation are given after the group of "Recollections," which includes the meditation upon the Breath, the Four Fundamentals of Attentiveness, etc.

The short formula permits one to practise a little meditation every day. It is also recited before beginning certain long meditations, such as the meditation on Respiration, for it "liberates the heart" from egoism.

In meditating upon Mettā, all thoughts of hostility or ill will are driven off, hate is put away. Before concentrating upon Love it is well to consider the evil of hate and of the actions inspired by enmity and to reflect upon the advantages of forbearance.

"Nothing forbearance doth excel" (Saṃyutta Nikāya: *Kindred Sayings*, i, 290).

"And it is with the object of *separating* the heart from enmity—the evil of which is discerned—and of *uniting* the heart with forbearance—the advantage of which is discerned—that the exercise of Love is to be begun." [1]

It is necessary to realize that all beings desire happiness, and to begin by wishing happiness for oneself; for no distinction should be made between oneself and other beings, and, moreover, one cannot radiate

As such subjects are more difficult for Western students, they are studied later on.

1 *Vide* Chapter ix of the *Visuddi-Magga* of Buddhaghosa, published by the Pali Text Society, and also separately published by the Buddhist Society of Great Britain and Ireland. All students should possess a copy—Luzac, 46 Great Russell Street, London.

love and happiness unless one possesses them.

The Mettā Sutta is so beautiful that it would be well to memorize it before studying the meditation formula.

MĒTTĀ SUTTA

(Sutta Nipāta No. 8)

This is what should be accomplished by the man who is wise, who seeks the good and has obtained peace:

Let him be strenuous, upright, and sincere, without pride, (easily) contented and joyous; let him not be submerged by the things of the world; let him not take upon himself the burden of riches; let his senses be controlled; let him be wise but not puffed up, and let him not desire great possessions (even) for his family.

Let him do nothing that is mean or that the wise would reprove.
May all beings be happy.
May they be joyous and live in safety.
All living beings, whether weak or strong,
In high, or middle, or low realms of existence,
Small or great, visible or invisible, near or far,
Born, or to be born,
May all beings be happy.

Let no one deceive another, nor despise any being
in any state; let none by anger or hatred wish harm
to another.

Even as a mother at the risk of her life watches over
and protects her only child, so with a boundless
mind [1] should one cherish all living things, suffusing love over the entire world, above, below, and
all around without limit; so let him cultivate an
infinite goodwill toward the whole world.

Standing or walking, sitting or lying down, during
all his waking hours let him cherish the thought
that this way of living is the best in the world.

Abandoning vain discussions, having a clear vision,
freed from sense appetites, he who is made perfect
will never again know rebirth.

METTĀ, *Short Practice-Plan*

To calm the mind and prepare it for concentration,
it is usually advisable for the student to practise the
breathing-exercises before attempting to meditate.

After reciting Ti Saraṇa, as in the Peace meditation,
begin by saying:

1. "A long breath I breathe in." ⎫
   "A long breath I breathe out." ⎬ 10 times
                                 ⎭

[1] Free from discrimination between oneself and others.

Then:

2. "A short breath I breathe in." ⎫
   "A short breath I breathe out." ⎬ 10 times
                                    ⎭

3. Let the breath regulate itself
   according to a rhythm which is
   natural and easy.

Simply observe the breath as it comes and goes, thinking of nothing else.

Then repeat mentally the short Mettā formula:

> May I be happy,
> May I preserve my happiness
> And live without enmity.

> May all beings,
> High or low,[1]
> Great or small,
> Strong or weak,
> Near or far,
> Visible or invisible,
> Be happy, preserve their happiness,
> And live without enmity.

Hold each of these thoughts (or phrases) for at least fifteen seconds in mind. Imagine the whole of one's nature filled with loving-kindness, and that

---

[1] Living on other planes or worlds, devas, pretas, etc.

there is no place for any other idea at all; continue until there is nothing but love pouring forth for all beings.

It may be well to say mentally:

> I am penetrated by love,
> Saturated with love,
> Absorbed in love.

Identify oneself with this love-thought

It is said that this state of mind is the best possible to maintain at all times and that "he sleeps happily, awakes happily, and dies unbewildered through the practice of emancipating the heart by love."

To develop and expand the Love meditation, the long formula should be employed.

METTĀ, *Long Formula*

Before beginning to practise the longer meditation, it is necessary to choose three persons to whom one will send thoughts of loving goodwill. These three persons should be living, and no one of them should tend to awaken passionate desire or lust.

1. Choose then a person who is very dear,
2. A person who inspires only indifference,
3. A person who is an adversary or an enemy.

Having these three persons clearly in mind, having

recited Ti Saraṇa and practised the breathing-exercises, begin by awakening thoughts of love for oneself. This makes four persons who should be considered as equally dear

THE FOUR PERSONS .

A

Oneself

Repeat mentally:

> May I be happy,
> May I preserve my happiness
> And live without enmity.
> My heart is full of loving-kindness.

B

To one who is dear

> I am sending loving thoughts to X,
> May he (or she) be happy,
> May he preserve his happiness,
> May he live without enmity.

Continue to surround and to bathe this person with pure, benevolent, loving thoughts.

C

To the indifferent person

I am sending loving thoughts to X,
May he (or she) be happy,
May he preserve his happiness,
May he live without enmity.

Send kindly, benevolent thoughts to this person. Continue to surround and bathe him with thoughts of goodwill, which will later break down indifference.

D

To the adversary

This person (X) has been unkind, unfriendly, or harmful to me. May I free myself of enmity toward him. May I free myself from anger.
May I wish him no hurt or harm,
May he be happy,
May he preserve his happiness,
May he live without enmity.

Do not fight, but refuse to harbour the disturbing feelings of resentment that the thought of an enemy may awaken.

For a few seconds say:

I am filled with goodwill,

I am nothing but goodwill.

Or:

I am making a thought of hatred to cease in the universe and so diminishing the force of hatred.

When calm, think again of this person, his good qualities, think of the suffering he is creating for himself (through bad Kamma) by his wrong actions. So arousing compassion in the heart, try again to send out thoughts of loving-kindness toward him.

When this meditation has been practised a number of times, success will be obtained.

"And now that he (the meditator) is again and again sending out love to four classes of persons, to himself, to the dear person, to the indifferent, and to the hostile . . . he should bring about a breaking down of all frontiers." [1]

Try to make no difference, no distinction, between oneself, the person dear, the indifferent person, and the adversary. Envelop them all in thoughts of love and goodwill *as if they were one person.*

Break down the boundaries between them by encircling them with love; try to create a composite

[1] "The breaking down of the barriers" (when love toward each and all is equal) gives rise to the love-image and to ecstasy.

image, superimposing one face upon the other, and to make no distinction between oneself and others.

One will become conscious of nothing but love when the barriers of personality are broken down; only a thought of love identified with the love-consciousness will exist. Continue to practise and develop this state of mind.

It is now time to enlarge the field of meditation and not to forget that all beings, not only man, must be surrounded by thoughts of loving goodwill.

METTĀ-BHĀVANĀ

Developing or expanding the love-formula,[1] send thoughts of love to the place one inhabits, the house, the country, and the continent.

Let the mind run over these divisions, pouring down thoughts of love, suffusing them with love, as one would a person who is dear.

BY QUARTERS

Imagine the globe divided into four quarters—

EAST	WEST	NORTH	SOUTH

Take each quarter in turn and imagine each as being dear. Pour down upon it thoughts of goodwill

[1] Beginners should not tire themselves by pursuing the meditation any farther, but as soon as sufficient training has been acquired, the love-formula is applied to the four quarters of the globe.

and of loving-kindness, as upon a person who is dear.
If it is of any help, imagine some fellow-being living
among the inhabitants of these quarters. Or imagine
that one is in the midst of these people, while thinking of each quarter in turn.

Repeat mentally:

May all beings in the East be happy,
May they preserve their happiness
And live without enmity.

May all beings in the West be happy . . . etc.

May all beings in the North be happy . . . etc.

May all beings in the South be happy,
May they preserve their happiness
And live without enmity.

So continue to suffuse one quarter of the globe with
thoughts accompanied by love; then the second quarter, then the third, and the fourth.

"Conscious of nothing but love, radiating love, he
covers each quarter and the four intermediate quarters
across by sections."

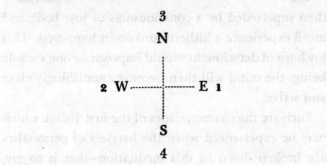

Again expand and develop the field of meditation to cover the Universe.

Send the "love-consciousness" circling around the globe, "as a horse turns around the circus rings."

Envelop the whole Universe radiating love, above, below, across everywhere. It is said: "The whole wide world of individual being, does he [the meditator] continue to suffuse with a loving consciousness, abounding, lofty, infinite, void of anger and ill will."

The breathing-exercises, long and short, may be repeated (and Ti Saraṇa recited by those who so desire) before coming out of the meditation, for it is not advisable suddenly to break off these higher states of consciousness.

Try to remember what one has thought, and felt, during meditation hours. A certain mental tranquillity should last over for some time.

An unusual sense of contentment is obtained and

then superseded by a consciousness of joy; body and mind experience a hitherto unknown happiness. This joy born of detachment should impregnate one's whole being, the mind will then become astonishingly clear and active.

Such are the characteristics of the first Jhāna, which may be experienced when the barriers of personality are broken down in this meditation—that is to say, when one succeeds in radiating thoughts of love *equally* toward all four persons. Later on, higher stages of ecstasy, including the Third Jhāna, may be obtained by this meditation [1] (Bhikkhu Nyānatiloka Thero).

II

KARUṆĀ

Compassion or Pity

Buddhist compassion is not a mere sentimental emotion. Meditating upon compassion awakens in the practiser an understanding of one of the principles of the Dhamma, *the fact of suffering, that is bound up with all phenomenal existence*. Moreover, pity is said to decrease the cruelty latent in human nature by softening the heart.

One should remember that all beings desire happi-

[1] *Vide* Chapter 7, "Jhānas."

ness, and that suffering (mental or physical) is inevitable, until the state of Nibbāṇa is attained through the conquest of desire and through *insight*, which is understanding perfected. For *ignorance*, in one form or another (and desire born of ignorance), is the cause of suffering.

It is well to bear in mind the unlimited compassion of the Enlightened One, the infinite pity for all beings that tormented his youth and led him to forsake everything in quest of the knowledge that would free humanity.

One should never lament or despair, but seek the light, cultivating and increasing intelligence and a boundless compassion for all creatures. In this way understanding is gained, intolerance is banished, and cruelty is diminished.

In the *Visuddhi-Magga* it is written: "As on seeing a person in poverty so does he [the meditator] suffuse all beings with pity [saying]: This person is in misery; would that he were free from suffering." Or: "Observing an evil-doer, pity is awakened, by thinking that his evil actions will lead him to states of suffering." Again, upon seeing someone who is prosperous, but selfish and hard-hearted, one reflects: "However much this person who is prosperous at present seems to be happy, he is to be pitied; for suffering will befall him owing to the absence of any good thoughts, words, or deeds," the three doors of action.

Pity is also "awakened by the thought that all beings are bound upon the wheel of Saṁsāra, wandering in the round of Birth and Death."

Having reflected upon all this, begin the meditation, if so desired, by repeating Ti Saraṇa and practising the breathing-exercises.

Consider the evil of hard-heartedness which leads to cruelty, and the virtue of compassion in the Universe, which not only frees the heart from egoism, but also diminishes suffering.

Then pity oneself for any suffering in one's own life, saying: "May I be happy, may I be free from suffering." In the same way pity any suffering in the life of the person who is very dear, wishing that he may be freed from suffering. Suffuse the indifferent person with compassion, wishing that he, too, may be free from suffering. Consider the enemy with compassion, wishing that he, also, may be free from suffering.

Make no distinction between oneself and the three other persons, pitying misfortune and the suffering caused by wrong desire (born of ignorance), saying: "May all beings escape from suffering."

Be conscious of nothing but an immense compassion.

Practise and develop the compassion-consciousness.

Suffuse the four quarters of the globe with compassion, taking each in turn, treating it as if one saw someone there who is in misery.

Encircle the whole world with the compassion-consciousness.[1]

End the meditation by making a resolution to assuage suffering, as far as possible, and to avoid inflicting suffering upon any living creature.

Repeat the breathing-exercises and Ti Saraṇa.

III

MUDITĀ

Sympathy with Happiness

The same plan that is used for meditation upon Mettā may be employed in developing Sympathetic Joy with the happiness of others.

In choosing the three persons, do not include anyone who is dead or anyone likely to arouse passion or lust. "A very dear person and, in due course, someone indifferent, and then an enemy. These are the three to be chosen."

This meditation frees or "liberates the heart from envy and jealousy and leads to contentment."

---

1 Those who are too depressed by thinking of suffering should now meditate upon Serenity.

The same degree of joy should be felt in the happiness of others as in one's own personal happiness.

There is always some joy, some happiness, abroad in the world; rejoice in this thought.

Think of the well-being and happiness that have already existed in the lives of the three persons chosen. Wish them future prosperity and happiness.

Begin by thinking of the joy and happiness in one's own life.

Thinking of the very dear person, rejoice in any happiness that has been his; wish him all joy, now and in the future.

Toward the indifferent person, conjure up the same sympathetic joy in any happiness that has been his, wishing him also a happy future.

The enemy must be treated in the same way. If, however, the thought of the enemy arouses envy or jealousy, reflect on the transitoriness of joy and happiness; realize how easily he may become unhappy, and that, in any case, he too, with the rest of us, is still dominated (more or less) by ignorance, which is always a source of suffering.

Thus thinking, one awakens compassion, and when one is pacified, let him send forth thoughts of sympathy to the enemy.

"Break down the barrier" between yourself and the three persons, until there is no distinction between these four persons, and nothing but *joyous sympathy with happiness remains*. Practise and develop this sentiment.

Divide the globe into four quarters, suffuse each quarter "as if it were a happy person," or imagine a happy person whom you love in this quarter.

Practise and develop as in the Mettā meditation.

Suffuse the whole wide world and all beings with sympathetic joy. Be conscious of nothing but sympathetic joy. Identify yourself with this sentiment.

IV

UPEKKHĀ

Equanimity or Serenity

Those who have perfected themselves in the Mettā and Muditā meditations are prepared to practise Equanimity or Serenity; they should realize that love and joy are transient emotions and that a state of Serenity is blessed.

Therefore one desires serenity for oneself and for others, being indifferent to pleasure and pain, realizing that both are impermanent. Equanimity gives one a foretaste of that peace which characterizes Nibbāna.

Try to imagine that the heart is penetrated by

Serenity, saturated with Serenity, absorbed in Serenity.

Among the three persons chosen, begin by thinking first of the indifferent person, for it is easier to think of such a one calmly.

Imagine him to be calm and serene; wish that he may attain and abide in Serenity.

Then, in the same way, calmly imagine a person who is dear as attaining Serenity.

Let an enemy then receive thoughts of Serenity; calm and indifferent, think of him as calm and serene.

Oneself, the dear one, the indifferent one, and the enemy must be looked upon with the same indifference with which one regards a neutral person.

"As on seeing a person neutral, neither lovable nor unlovable, he [the meditator] *would be even-minded, so he suffuses all beings with even-mindedness."* [1]

Practising and developing the meditation, suffuse the quarters, and then the globe, with Serenity.

Imagine that all is serene and that one is conscious of nothing but Serenity.

The breathing-exercises and Ti Saraṇa may be used to begin and to end this meditation.

[1] *Visuddhi-Magga.*

11

MEDITATION UPON
THE FOUR FUNDAMENTALS OF
ATTENTIVENESS

MAHĀ SATIPATTHĀNA SUTTA (MAHĀ VAGGA)

THE study of the meditation of the Four Fundamentals of Attentiveness is most important. It is essential, for concentration-training, to learn to observe the principal activities of the body and the mind.

"Mindfulness as to the Body" is one of the basic meditations practised even by young girls in Buddhist convents, such as one finds in Kandy, Ceylon, "because," as the Theri (the elder sister) explained, "body is all they know." This meditation proceeds by reasoning from the known to the unknown.

It is said that the Buddha (before his enlightenment), while he was still a Bodhisatta, trained himself to observe attentively the external phenomena of the Universe, as well as the inner workings of the body and the mind.

By means of this meditation we may verify one of the Four Noble Truths—Impermanence, which characterizes all forms of existence. As soon as this has been understood, one begins to be detached from the illusions of the senses. Later on, the desire to search for Reality is awakened.

One should bear in mind that Buddhists consider the unstable, the impermanent, that which is eternally becoming, perpetually changing, as unable to ensure any lasting happiness.

The meditation on the Four Fundamentals should teach us to understand that our personalities, composed of sensations, emotions, thoughts, and so forth, are never for two moments the same. The component parts of the "Self," or individual, are fleeting and impermanent. How, then, can the ego, which is only the sum total of these associated components, be permanent? [1]

Such a conclusion is discouraging to the egocentric, the selfish man, but will not trouble anyone who has understood the *unity* of all life beneath the diversity of forms, since he knows that an escape, a deliverance from the limitation of personality, is to be found upon the transcendental plane of Nibbāṇa.

Thus meditating, one becomes detached from this and that; one escapes from the tyranny and error of

[1] *Vide* Khandha, "Pali Terms."

sense impressions; consciousness is purified and fortified.

This particular concentration teaches one to observe the contents of one's mind, the tendencies of one's character, so that one may control and purify oneself.

The Four Fundamentals which should be attentively observed are:

BODY (KĀYA)

1. Observation, or contemplation, of the Body: taking Breathing as one of the essential functions of the Body, which is easily observed.[1]
2. Observation, or contemplation, of Feelings (i.e., sensations and emotions).

MIND (CITTA)

3. Observation, or contemplation, of Thoughts (as they arise and subside).
4. Observation, or contemplation, of Internal Phenomena (A and B).

A

The five hindrances to meditation are:

[1] Breathing is controlled both by the conscious brain and by the subconscious sympathetic nervous system.

(1) Sensual desire; (2) Ill will; (3) Sloth or dullness; (4) Restless brooding; (5) Doubt.

The student should find out which of these demeritorious (Akusala) states of mind is present, observe it, then find out which of these states is absent.

B

He should also find out and observe the meritorious (Kusala) thoughts present in the mind:

(1) Attentiveness; (2) Desire to investigate the Law or Teaching (Dhamma); (3) Energy; (4) Keen interest (Joyful comprehension); (5) Tranquillity; (6) Concentration; (7) Equanimity (Serenity).

He should remember what is said in the *Dhammapada* of pure and impure thoughts and their influence upon the conditions of life.

"All things are the result of thought; founded on thought; created by thought. If a man speaks or acts with an impure mind, suffering follows him as the wheel follows the hoof of the ox that draws the cart."

"All things are the result of thought; founded on thought; created by thought. If a man speaks or acts with a purified mind, happiness follows him as closely as his never-departing shadow." (*Dhammapada* 1–2)

PRACTICE-PLAN

OBSERVATION OF THE BODY (KĀYA) [1]

I. Breathing

The breathing should be observed *objectively*, not as if it were the breathing of the person meditating, but as if it were some external phenomenon (a life-process) that one is observing.

This is the most important part of this meditation.

"The entire aim of the practice is to impress the student with the fact that the process that is going on resembles all other processes taking place in the Universe, which in their totality constitute the so-called Universe at any given moment."

"This process, like every other process in the body, is not owned, possessed, or directed by a Self or Ego."

To abolish all notions of separateness, one should cultivate the habit not only of observing impersonally, but of thinking: *"There is breathing, there is hunger, there is thirst,"* instead of: *"I breathe . . ."* etc.

Begin the meditation by observing the breath as exhaled and inhaled; let the mind follow it, watch the process, saying (mentally):

[1] *Vide* Dr. B. E. Fernando in the *British Buddhist*, Vol. VII, Nos. 7 and 8.

"There is breathing here," as consciously one continues—

Breathing out a long breath }
Breathing in a long breath } 10 times

Then—

Breathing out a short breath }
Breathing in a short breath } 10 times

Watch the process.

Clearly conscious, try to observe the whole course of the breath, the higher, middle, and lower breathing,[1] exhaling and inhaling ten times.

Calming this physical function, continue to breathe out and in, equalizing, "smoothing," the breathing.

Thus contemplating a function of the body, or bodies, one should learn that:

"Body is a part of the general mass of matter in the Universe."

II. Observation of Sensations and Emotions

Observe the Feelings.

Scrutinize each sensation, pleasant or unpleasant, as it is produced by impact upon any one of the sense organs, saying (mentally):

[1] *Vide* "Anāpāna Sati," Chapter 13.

"There is feeling here,"

"There is a sensation $\left\{\begin{array}{c}\text{pleasant}\\ \text{or}\\ \text{unpleasant.}\end{array}\right\}$ It $\left\{\begin{array}{c}\text{arises}\\ \text{increases}\\ \text{diminishes}\\ \text{disappears."}\end{array}\right.$

Follow its course, analyse, etc.

Note that *All Sensations are Impermanent.*

Observe the Emotions in the same way, saying (mentally):

"There is an emotion $\left\{\begin{array}{c}\text{pleasant}\\ \text{or}\\ \text{unpleasant.}\end{array}\right\}$ It $\left\{\begin{array}{c}\text{arises}\\ \text{increases}\\ \text{diminishes}\\ \text{disappears."}\end{array}\right.$

All Emotions are Impermanent.[1]

"It is not intended to deny that all feelings are not alike in different persons, but to teach us that ultimately there is no separate self [2] owning, operating, carrying on these bodies (yours, mine) and their functions. When we understand this, sooner or later, we obtain liberation 'from the passing show,' and realize Nibbāna."

---

[1] Call to mind an emotion which in other days caused intense suffering and which today leaves one completely indifferent.
[2] Unchanging separate Ego. Each man is an integral part of the Universe, says the Master of the Law Tai-Hsu.

III. Observation of Mind (Citta)

Observe one's thoughts impersonally as they arise, increase, and subside—demeritorious thoughts full of craving, hatred, and delusion, or noble thoughts that are meritorious—saying:

"Here a thought of hatred arises, increases, diminishes, and disappears,"
or—

"A noble thought arises, increases, diminishes, and disappears."

All Thoughts are Impermanent.

"We should train ourselves to regard our thoughts purely objectively, as we observe any other phenomena in the Universe—rain, thunder, etc."—"The aim is to overcome the common notion that a certain little separate self, or Ego, is thinking and to realize the truth that thought is simply occurring"; that is to say:

"Thoughts are a part of the general process of the Universe." [1]

"By practising this introspection attentively, we should attain the ending of sorrow, which means the ending of separateness, discriminations, distinctions of self, and all ideas of personality or individuality."

[1] Just as Body is part of the general matter of the Universe.

In other words, we shall reach a state of *selflessness* free from all egoism.

IV. *Observation of the Hindrances*

A. *Demeritorious States of Mind*

Observe the presence in oneself of the five states of mind which keep alive a sense of separateness, hamper our progress, and hinder meditation.

Present?
or
Absent?

{
Sensual desire (lust),
Ill will,
Sloth (dullness, or lack of energy in following the Path),
Restless brooding, agitation of mind,
Doubt, as to the teaching of the Buddha.
}

Note which is present, which is absent, but always observe impersonally, saying:

"Lust is present (or absent).

"Ill will is present (or absent)," etc.

Banish the demeritorious state. Do not blame oneself. Withdraw the attention from it and concentrate upon the opposite state; if lust is present, think: Purity, saying:

"I am making a thought of lust (or ill will, etc.) *cease in the Universe."*

Do not say: "I am destroying a lustful thought in

myself," but "in the Universe."

B. *Meritorious States of Mind*

Observe the presence of meritorious states of mind.

Present?
or
Absent?
{
Attentiveness,
Desire to investigate the Law or Teaching (Dhamma),
Energy,
Keen interest (Joyful comprehension),
Tranquillity,
Concentration,
Equanimity.
}

Note carefully which is present, or absent; do not say: "in my mind," but simply: "There is attentiveness, investigation . . ." etc. Always observe these states objectively, impersonally, as one observes any other phenomena in the Universe of which they are processes.

All Sensations, Emotions, and Thoughts are Impermanent.

The visible Universe (which the senses register) is nothing but a perpetual flux of phenomena whose material aggregates are unreal [1] since all phenomena

---

[1] Or of only an apparent reality. Remember that because there is "an unborn, uncreated, unmade, unformed" (*Udāna,* viii), we can escape from the phenomenal and attain reality beyond change. Seeing impermanence in all things around us and within us awakens the desire for the Permanent, beyond the phenomenal.

are unstable, impermanent, and eternally in a state
of becoming.

12

MEDITATION UPON "THE SELF"

"Truth the Second tells of Suffering's cause: how this lies in Desire, in Self-desire alone; how, because all living beings will set up for themselves a Self in opposition to the whole great Life whereunto they belong; will work and lust and live not for all life at large, but for their fancied Self alone—Suffering follows them from life to life, until at last they learn life's highest lesson; until they cast out Self and its desires completely, and live and work at last for Life unlimited." [1]

MEDITATION ON "THE SELF" [2]

THE meditator first cultivates (at the outset) "Purity of vision" in order to comprehend things as they really are. With his mind concentrated (one-pointed) he scrutinizes his "self" and after due examination discovers that his personality is nothing but a mere composition of mind and matter, the former consisting of volitional activities (that arise as the result of the senses coming in contact with sense stimuli), and the latter (matter) composed of forces and qualities that manifest themselves in multifarious phenomena.

[1] *The Wisdom of the Aryas*, by Allan Bennett (Ananda M.). E. P. Dutton & Co., New York, 1923.
[2] From the treatise on Nibbāṇa by the Bhikkhu Nārada Thero, pp. 24 et seq.

The Causes of Personality

Having thus gained a correct view of the real nature of his "self," freed from the false notion of an identical substance of mind and matter, he attempts to investigate the cause of this personality (self, or Ego).

He realizes that everything in the world, himself not excluded, is conditioned by some cause or causes, past or present, and that his existence is due to past: (1) ignorance, (2) craving, (3) attachment, (4) Kamma,[1] and (5) to the physical nourishment of the present life. This personality (self) has arisen on account of these five causes. Just as the past activities have conditioned the present, so the present will condition the future.

Meditating thus, he transcends all doubts with regard to past, present, and future.[2] He then understands that all conditioned things are transient (anicca), subject to suffering (dukkha), and devoid of any immortal soul (anattā).[3] Wherever he turns his eyes he sees naught but these three characteristics. He comprehends that life is merely a flux,[4] a continuous undivided movement. Neither in heaven nor on earth does he find any genuine happiness, for every form of

1 Kamma, action and the result of action.
2 He sees how one conditions the others.
3 Devoid of any self substance.
4 A stream.

pleasure is only a prelude to pain. That which is transient (impermanent) is therefore painful, and where change and sorrow prevail there cannot be a permanent Ego (since this Ego is ever changing in all its component parts).

Aura

As he is absorbed in meditation one day, to his surprise, he perceives an aura emanating from his body, he experiences a pleasure hitherto unknown, happiness and quietude.

He becomes even-minded and strenuous, his religious fervour increases, his attentiveness is perfected, his insight extraordinarily keen. He imagines that he has attained saintship; this misconception is principally due to the aura; he ardently desires this state of mind.

He soon realizes that these temptations are only defilements (hindrances) to insight, and that he has not really acquired saintship. Therefore he endeavours to distinguish between the right and the wrong path.

The Arising and Disappearing of Phenomena

Perceiving the right path he resumes his meditation, concentrating his attention on the *arising and the passing away* of conditioned things (phenomena). Of these two characteristics the latter [1] becomes impressed upon his mind, because change is more conspicuous than becoming. Therefore he observes the dissolution of all things. He perceives that both mind and matter, which constitute personality, are in a state of constant flux, never identical during any two consecutive moments. To him comes the knowledge (the understanding) that this dissolution is fearful. The whole world appears to him to resemble a pit of burning embers—a source of danger.

Consequently he reflects on the wretchedness and vanity of this fearful and wicked world and, feeling disgusted with it, he desires to escape.[2]

Detachment

With this object in view, he again meditates upon the three characteristics (of existence) and then becomes completely indifferent to all conditioned things, harbouring neither attachment nor aversion for anything in the world (any worldly object). Having reached this stage of mental culture, he takes for his object (of concentration) one of the three characteristics that particularly attracts him, and he continues intently to develop insight, reflecting upon that char-

---

[1] Passing away, change, dissolution, the end, is more easily observed than the origin.

[2] From the phenomenal and to reach the transcendental state of Nibbāṇa.

acteristic, until, to his indescribable joy, the glorious
day arrives when he, for the first time, realizes [1] Nibbāna, his ultimate goal.

PRACTICE-PLAN

Recite Ti Saraṇa—the Three Refuges.

Half close the eyes—concentrating the attention at
a point between the eyebrows.

Practise the breathing-exercises as indicated in the
Peace meditation for beginners:

1. Exhale and inhale ten times (breathing long, deep
   breaths).
2. Exhale and inhale ten times (breathing short quick
   breaths).
3. Let the breathing take its normal course—observing
   the breaths as they come and go.

Or—

Advanced students may follow the exercises indicated in *Ānāpāna* meditation.[2]

---

[1] In a flash of intuition he glimpses Nibbāna, realizes what it might
be. This is the experience of the Sotāpanna, Stream-Winner, and this
reoccurs at the entrance to each of the three other paths.

[2] "Ānāpāna Sati," Chapter 13.— (1) Follow the counts breathing out
and in a long breath, then a short breath; (2) then follow the
course of the breath; (3) concentrate on the contact of the air with
the nostrils.

Examination

Examine that which is called the "Self," the personality.

It is composed of nothing but mind and matter.

Mind is the result of volitional activities that arise as the result of the senses coming in contact with sense stimuli.

Matter (body) is nothing but the result of forces and qualities manifested in phenomena.

A

Seek out the cause of personality.

All things, personality included, spring from and are conditioned by a cause or causes.

The existence of a "self" is due to:

1. Ignorance in the past; from ignorance desire is born;
2. Craving (for phenomenal existence);
3. Attachment (to life, persons, and things);
4. Kamma (action, the result of thought and action in the past);
5. Food absorbed in this life.

Personality is the result of these five causes.

B

The thoughts,
the deeds,
and acts of this present life will condition future lives.

C

All conditioned things are:

1. Impermanent,
2. Unsatisfactory (there is no absolute enduring happiness),
3. Void of any eternal changeless entity (that is, Ego)
   —since all that goes to make up this personality is constantly changing.

Hence,

Life is a continuous flux,
a unique stream having continuous, undivided movement.[1]

THE ARISING AND PASSING AWAY OF PHENOMENA

A

Contemplate the decline and dissolution [2] of the

---

[1] Unity of life in diversity of form. Between the "self" of one life and another, or even the "self" of today and yesterday, there is *continuity*, but it is not *exactly* the same during any two moments.
[2] The passing away (or death) is apparent, striking, and so more easily observed than the arising.

thoughts and the body (mind and matter) constituting the "self" or personality, saying (mentally):

Decay is inherent in all compounded things, doomed to dissolution.

Phenomenal life is as unstable and shifting as quicksand,

it resembles a burning pit,

it is full of snares and suffering,

there is no sure foothold here.

B

Aversion to the phenomenal will then arise and engender the desire to escape from the limitations of personality.

INDIFFERENCE AND DETACHMENT

A

Meditating thus, one becomes indifferent to phenomenal life and the striving of "self."

To become detached, meditate upon the three characteristics of existence:

1. Impermanence;
2. Suffering (physical or mental, or mere irritability);
3. Egolessness—observing that the "self" is always changing.

B

Concentrate upon any one of these three characteristics, having chosen the most suitable.[1]

If it is Impermanence, keep on saying (mentally):
All things are impermanent.
Everything around us is impermanent.
Everything within us (thoughts, sensations, etc.) is impermanent.

Cultivate insight as to impermanence.

Continue until there is

$\left. \begin{array}{l} \text{no attraction} \\ \text{no aversion} \end{array} \right\}$ for any conditioned state or object.

Through detachment, the capacity to look upon all things impersonally is acquired; this leads to serenity and to that peace which is a foretaste of Nibbāṇa.

Return

It is not advisable to break off a meditation abruptly, as it may produce a shock. Therefore practise the respiration exercises backward.
Exhaling and inhaling short breaths ten times.
Exhaling and inhaling long breaths ten times.
Normal breathing.
Open the eyes.
Recite Ti Saraṇa (the Three Refuges).

[1] Impermanence is a suitable subject for everyone. Suffering is too depressing for certain natures to meditate upon.

13

MEDITATION UPON RESPIRATION

ĀNĀPĀNA SATI

Résumé of a treatise[1] by Dr. Cassius Pereira, L.R.C.P. London, M.R.C.S. Eng.
Practice Plans
Text of Sutta 118 M.N.
Extracts from the chief Commentaries of Buddhaghosa, Chapter viii (IX Div.), of the *Visuddhi-Magga*.

ĀNĀPĀNA SATI

Attentive Observation of Respiration

THE meditation on Respiration is considered to be of the greatest importance. It is placed last in our list as it is likely to prove the most difficult for Western students because of its subtlety.

Dr. Cassius Pereira's treatise on *Ānāpāna Sati* is the result of his personal experience, and of his observations in directing classes of meditation in Ceylon. It should therefore help students who seriously wish to study those traditional practices which have sur-

[1] *Meditation Based on Mindfulness with Regard to Breathing* (Bastian and Co., Colombo).

vived through the centuries and which are still valuable in Buddhist training. In making a résumé of the essential instructions of Dr. Cassius Pereira, his own words have been quoted, as far as possible, in this version, which is necessarily condensed.

The famous text of *The Path of Purity (Visuddhi-Magga)* in its English translation is considered by the Bhikkhus to be obscure and at times incorrect. A new translation, from the Pāli, of the eighth chapter, with the comments of Buddhaghosa, is given; it has been carefully supervised by the Ven. P. Vajirañāṇa Thero of Ceylon.

While observing attentively the outgoing and incoming breaths, as soon as concentration has been established, the student contemplates a whole series of subjects.

(1) Body (kāya); [1] (2) Sentiments: Joy (pīti), Happiness (sukha); (3) Mind; (4) Phenomena, and the cessation of this and that state; when the transitory nature of all phenomena has been realized, the three characterstics of phenomenal existence, Anicca, Dukkha, Anattā, are thoroughly meditated and liberation may then be obtained.

This meditation is a perfect example of the Bud-

[1] Body in the First Tetrad, Sentiments in the Second Tetrad, etc. Note the relationship between this meditation and the Four Fundamentals of Attentiveness.

dhist quest for supreme knowledge, which is gradually acquired through insight.

For, depending upon no one but himself, through his own efforts and insight the Buddhist reaches self-liberation.

RÉSUMÉ OF DR. CASSIUS PEREIRA'S STUDY OF ĀNĀPĀNA SATI [1]

There are eight stages in the practice:

1. Counting (Gananā)—i.e., of the exhaled and inhaled breaths.
2. Following (Anubandhanā)—i.e., the thought pursues the breath.
3. Mindfulness of contact of breath (Phusanā)—the contact of the breath with the nostrils or the lips.
4. Watching (Ṭhapana), without paying attention to the breath.[2]
5. Realizing the Transitoriness (Sallakkhaṇā) of respiration.
6. Path (Magga) Reflection (Vavatthāna).
7. Fruit (Phala) Reflection (Pārisuddhi).
8. Contemplation Reflection (Paṭipassana) on all this.[3]

---

[1] This meditation on Breathing is one of the forty Kammaṭṭhānas (subjects of meditation) of the Theravāda school.

[2] Be aware that breathing is taking place, but without paying particular attention to it.

[3] It is not proposed to deal here with the last four stages. One stage leads to the next, and he who has accomplished the first four is highly advanced. (C. P.)

Preparation

Having taken one's food and rested awhile to be free from subsequent drowsiness; having bathed and put on clean, comfortable clothing, putting away all distracting thoughts of business or family and all worries and doubts, one retires to the chosen place of meditation, a quiet spot,[1] and sits down on the prepared seat facing East.

It is necessary to choose a comfortable position, keeping the head erect, the spinal column straight. The breathing should be easy.[2]

Mettā

One begins by sending benevolent thoughts to all beings—high or low, great or small, near or far, visible or invisible—wishing that they may be happy, keep their happiness, and live without enmity.

Then putting aside pride and self-delusion (with compassionate, calm, trustful, and devoted mind), one reflects on the incomparable virtues of the Triple Gem (Ti Saraṇa):[3] the Buddha, the Law, the Order. One now recollects all that has been said of this

---

[1] "Beneath a secluded tree, a thousand paces in the jungle," a cave, etc. Complete silence is necessary; noise is more disturbing to this meditation than to any other.

[2] The classic position of the ancients is usually too difficult and would only inconvenience those who are not used to it.

[3] *Vide* Ti Saraṇa, "Pāli Terms."

meditation, its glory, greatness, the stages, and the outcome thereof.[1]

I. First Stage: *Counting (Gananā)*

This is the stage associated with counting. One concentrates upon the breathing, noting whether the breaths be long or short and, later on, rapid, feeble, until at last they are apparently absent.[2]

Beginners should not count less than five or more than ten. The aspirant (Yogāvacara) [3] chooses a certain number and adheres to it during the entire practice.

Count one for inhaling, two for exhaling, etc.

At first let the count be at the close of the breath—that is, having inhaled, mark one; having exhaled, mark two.

Later on, when the method has been mastered, instead of counting at the close of the breath, count one at the beginning of inhaling and two at the beginning of the exhaling.[4]

---

[1] According to tradition, it is glorious as having been the meditation practised by the Buddha at the moment of Enlightenment.

[2] Observe the breathing, and note attentively the variations produced while seeking concentration (one-pointedness of mind). Ānāpāna Sati is the observation of breathing which has two phases—exhaling and inhaling.

[3] Yogāvacara, the aspirant, in this case the person practising. See "Pāli Terms."

[4] Usually exhaling precedes inhaling in practising Ānāpāna Sati. See *Visuddhi-Magga*. (G. C. L.)

Dr. Cassius Pereira says: "Counting should be continued as long as necessary; that is to say, until the mind is so concentrated that it thinks of nothing but breath, without the aid of counting."

I have found the instructions of Dr. Cassius Pereira difficult, and so, in my classes, I follow the counting used in the Peace meditation.

First taking a long breath—

Inhale counting   1   2   3   4   5 ⎫
                                      ⎬ 10 times
Exhale counting   1   2   3   4   5 ⎭

At the end of each complete breath (inhaling—exhaling) mark one, until this has been counted ten times. Then, taking a short breath, repeat the same exercises ten times. Establish normal breathing, continuing to mark the count at the end of each complete breath, simply observing the process. (G. C. L.)

II. SECOND STAGE: *The Course of the Breath (Anubandhanā)*

When counting can be dispensed with, the second stage has been reached. To prevent the mind from wandering, let it follow the course of the breath in its passages through the nostrils [1] and the chest (or thorax) as far down as the navel. Follow the return of the breath from the navel, through the thorax and the nostrils.

The nostrils and the navel are the limits (Sīmā) which are not to be overstepped.[2] When this practice

[1] Ghānadvāra: literally Nose-door.
[2] Do not go beyond these limits as one does in certain Yogic practices.

is perfected, the observation of the course of the breath becomes automatic.

III. THIRD STAGE: *Contact (Phusanā)*

This stage is associated with contact. The object of concentration is the contact of the breath with the nostrils.

The attention should be concentrated upon the breath at the precise moment when it enters or leaves the nostrils.

The mind is not permitted to follow the breath, but only to note the entrance and exit of the breath through the nostrils. However, the mind is automatically conscious of the whole course without paying attention to it.

The nostrils are called the "closely helpful object" (Upanibandhanā nimitta) for obtaining concentration.

The essential thing (Padhāna) is the fitness (Viriya) of the Yogāvacara for those exercises; in the following (the fourth) stage the five hindrances are inhibited, false reasoning is precluded, the trances are gained.

When this occurs, the mind is no longer concentrated upon the breath or upon the nostrils; it is calm in trance.[1]

[1] This really happens in the fourth stage. (G. C. L.)

The great difference between the Ānāpāna Sati meditation and the other meditations is that *here* the object of concentration, "Breath," instead of becoming more and more vivid (as is usual), is gradually lost sight of.

Because the Yogāvacara has trained his body and mind in the practice of morality and of repeated meditation, he attains a state of purity and lightness. He gently glides into finer and finer breathing. He is still aware of this, but at last he becomes unconscious of any breathing at all.

This happens before trance is gained, and the practice must not be relinquished. He asks himself:

"Who does not breathe?
Who breathes?
Where does breath reside?"

A fœtus does not breathe, for it is immersed in fluid.
A person who is asphyxiated does not breathe.
In the Fourth Jhāna, breathing is suspended.
The dead are devoid of breath.
Beings in the celestial Rūpa and Arūpa realms do not breathe, nor does the saint in Nirodha samāpatti.[1]

Since one is not at present in any of these states, one breathes, but *the breathing is too subtle to be observed.*

[1] Nirodha samāpatti: attainment of cessation.

Three thoughts are present:

1. The thought of inhalation,
2. The thought of exhalation,
3. The thought of the nostrils.

The help of all these is necessary for the attainment of trance-vicinity concentration (Upacāra samādhi) and, later on, of full trance concentration (Appanā samādhi). But the presence of these thoughts is not conducive to concentration (that is, "one-pointedness of mind"), and Ānāpāna Sati cannot be one-thought, since the word means outbreathing and inbreathing.

Now that the breathing has apparently ceased, the three thoughts (inhaling, exhaling, and contact) are combined in one thought [1]—that of Breath. This continues until the meditation leads to the acquirement of what is called the "after-image" (Patibhāga Nimitta).

The meditation should be reinstated. "Where does the breath strike?"

It strikes the nostrils.

This is taken (again) as the object of concentration.

Therefore in the third stage, as it advances, there is no suspended breath (in reality), but our senses are not sufficiently acute to perceive the subtle breathing.

[1] "Seem to be one" (C.P.), but the practiser, no longer feeling his breathing, is troubled; so he concentrates once more on the nostrils, where the breath strikes, for this is the original point of contact.

This condition of apparently suspended breath corresponds to the acquired sign (Uggaha Nimitta) of other Kammaṭṭhānas, but this is still a preliminary stage of concentration (Parikamma samādhi). Soon, perhaps before many days elapse, the "after-image" of breath (Patibhāga Nimitta) will appear. With the arising of this image the fourth stage begins.[1]

IV. FOURTH STAGE: *(Ṭhapana)*

The fourth stage is associated with the "after-image" (Patibhāga Nimitta) and does not begin until this has been acquired.[2]

This image, or sign, as it is sometimes called, has not the same appearance to everyone. "The aspect of the phenomena depends entirely on the ideas and cognizing power of the practiser." It is the "cognizing faculty" that causes the image to be seen under different aspects.

[1] "The condition of seemingly suspended breaths is equivalent to the 'acquired sign' (Uggaha Nimitta) of other Kammaṭṭhānas. The practiser is still at 'preliminary concentration' (Parikamma samādhi) though he has risen above his 'original sign' (Parikamma nimitta), i.e. the breaths. The 'acquired mark' (Uggaha nimitta) is thus attained, and soon, perchance before many days elapse, the 'after-image' (Patibhāga nimitta) is also attained." (Dr. Cassius A. Pereira.)

[2] The acquired image is the image of the object of meditation when it is seen just as vividly with the eyes closed as open. The after-image is a more subtle form of the acquired image transposed in the mind. There arises in the mind of the practiser an image of Breath; he concentrates all his attention upon it; some see it as a cobweb, others as a soap bubble, a mist, etc. (G. C. L.)

"In other words, its appearance depends on the character and the knowledge of the person practising the meditation. When the 'after-image,' with the trance-vicinity concentration (Upacāra samādhi) that accompanies it, has been obtained, the Yogāvacara has passed the preliminary stage of concentration. But he is still in the Sphere of the Senses (Kāmāvacara). At this point it is advisable, if possible, to consult an instructor (Guru)."

From now on the "after-image" *becomes the object of concentration,* whereas the "breath" and the "nostrils" have hitherto served this purpose.

With the attainment of this stage (while in trance-vicinity concentration) the five Hindrances (Nīvaraṇā) to meditation: lust, anger, dullness or sloth, restless broodings, and doubts, are temporarily suppressed. All craving is absent, and the mind is calm. These events take place simultaneously.

The practiser must constantly keep the after-image in mind, but he is not advised to reflect on any of its details, such as form, colour, etc.

He must cherish and enlarge the image until it seems to fill all space. As concentration increases, "full trance concentration (Appanā samādhi)," the first stage of Jhāna, is attained.[1]

[1] *Vide: Visuddhi-Magga.* When the after-image has been acquired, the contemplation of the Body and the Mind is practised in the First Tetrad. In the First Jhāna, analysis, reflection, joy, happiness, and concentration are present.

This state of "full trance," transcending the sense planes (Kāmāvacara), leads to the plane of Pure Form (Rūpāvacara).

Full trance is to be cultivated to perfect:

1. The power of instantaneous reflection;
2. The power of instantaneous attainment;
3. The power of instantaneous reaction;
4. The power of compelling anything desired to take place, through sheer force of will;
5. The power of reflection and investigation.

When the training in meditation has been perfected, *it will not be necessary* to start with counting and go through all the stages to attain ecstasy. It is possible to enter into the First Jhāna at will. It is essential, however, to maintain a state of absolutely pure morality (Sīla visuddhi). "There must be no lust, cruelty, anger, harshness, or envy in the meditator who wishes to preserve these powers unimpaired."

The state of Jhāna samāpatti may be prolonged at will. The Buddhist sees no advantage in extending this trance beyond seven days.

It is now necessary to equalize mental forces (indriya samatta paṭipādanatā): confidence, energy, mindfulness, concentration, and wisdom; these forces must be well balanced.

Continuing the meditation, one attains higher

trances (up to the fourth). It is now possible to attain the four higher trances on the Fòrmless planes (Arū-pāvacara), although it is profitless. Even though a supranormal state has been reached, this state is still mundane (lokiya—of the world). The keen trance mind is able to penetrate the true nature of things, by meditating on Impermanence, Suffering, and the non-Ego. A flash of intuition, or insight (Vipassanā), gives the Yogāvacara his first glimpse of the supramundane (lokuttara) plane. This is the "insight" of the Stream-winner—Sotapatti maggañāṇa. In this stage, false views (the illusion of a permanent self), doubts, and belief in Rites ánd Ceremonies (as efficacious) are abolished for ever. Henceforth birth in the various realms of Suffering (Preta loka, animal kingdoms, etc.) is no longer possible.

The experience of even the First Jhāna is that of divine happiness. To attain the supramundane by this method of insight, it is necessary to emerge from the "full trance (appanā)" and return to "trance vicinity (Upacāra samādhi)," the preliminary stage of concentration.

Vipassanā (insight), which the Buddhist seeks, is the threshold of the ultramundane plane (lokuttara) because it leads out of the cosmic plane (lokiya) to ineffable and permanent Peace. Insight is seeing existence as it really is. When the "great awakening" comes, all this seeming reality (of ordinary worldly life) will prove to be of the same stuff that dreams are made of.

Before the Yogāvacara attains Enlightenment, four flashes of intuition [1] precede the "great awakening." Penetrating insight dissipates the whole illusion.

Seeing life as it is in reality, realizing Impermanence in all things, the Yogāvacara seeks to attain the Permanent, and progresses by the four higher stages of the meditation toward the Goal.

Purity of life and purity of thought have already been cultivated; in the last four stages additional "purities" must be perfected:

1. Right understanding,
2. The transcending of doubt,
3. Discerning the true paths,
4. Progressive discerning,
5. Purity of Insight itself.

The Yogāvacara, advancing step by step toward the light of the fully awakened and toward the total destruction of craving and thirst (Taṇhā), may attain the enjoyment of sustained cessation (Nirodha samāpatti).

[1] These four flashes are associated with the four corresponding paths: those of the (1) Sotāpanna; (2) Sakadāgāmim; (3) Anāgāmim; (4) Arahat. *Vide* p. 67: "The Four Paths."

The bliss and absolute freedom of Nibbāṇa may be experienced even in this terrestrial existence.

SHORT PRACTICE-PLAN

To familiarize students with the breathing-exercises used in meditating Ānāpāna Sati, it will be advisable to follow the short practice-plan before undertaking the longer classic meditation, which is difficult (if not impossible) unless one has mastered the different stages of respiration. I have used the usual system of counting as likely to be familiar to students of this book and easiest for Westerners.

Preparation

Begin by reciting the short Love-formula, as in the longer Ānāpāna Sati meditation, saying:

"May I be happy, free from suffering;
May I keep my happiness and live without enmity.
May all beings,
High or low,
Big or little,
Weak or strong,
Near or far,
Visible or invisible,
Be happy, free from suffering;
May they keep their happiness
And live without enmity."

Ti Sarana

Recite the Three Refuges (three times).[1]

I. Counting

"I breathe out a long breath."
$\underset{1}{}\quad\underset{2}{}\quad\underset{3}{}\quad\underset{4}{}\quad\underset{5}{}$

"I breathe in a long breath."
$\underset{1}{}\quad\underset{2}{}\quad\underset{3}{}\quad\underset{4}{}\quad\underset{5}{}$

} 10 times

1   2   3   4   5

1   2   3   4   5

Ten counts exhaling and inhaling, ten times, will make one hundred counts.

"I breathe out a short breath."

1 2 3 4 5

"I breathe in a short breath."

1 2 3 4 5

} 10 times

II. The Course of the Breath

Exhaling, follow the course of the breath
up from the navel,
through the thorax,
and out through the nostrils.

Inhaling, follow the course of the breath
in through the nostrils,

---

1 Buddhaṁ saraṇaṁ gacchāmi.
Dhammaṁ saraṇaṁ gacchāmi.
Saṅghaṁ saraṇaṁ gacchāmi.

through the thorax,
as far down as the navel.

Exhaling and inhaling ten times—do not follow the counts, but just the *course* of the breath.

III. Contact

Think only of the contact of the air with the nostrils
("nose-door") while:

Exhaling and inhaling ten times, saying:

"*The breath touches (strikes) the nostrils* as I breathe
out."
"The breath strikes the nostrils as I breathe in."

Repeat mentally:

> "I breathe,
> Breath is in me,
> I am nothing but breath,
> There is breathing,
> Breath is everywhere,
> Nothing but breath,
> All is breath."

IV. The Image

Sooner or later a mental image of the breath arises in the mind. Let it grow and enlarge until it seems to fill all space. Concentrate upon it.

Do not be troubled if the image does not appear. Some obtain it fairly quickly, others only after a long time.

Concentrating upon the image, one may practise the longer [1] Ānāpāna Sati meditation. (See text of the *Visuddhi-Magga* long formula.)

RETURN

One may follow the meditation backward step by step if one likes, saying:

"All is breath,
Nothing but breath,
Breath is everywhere,
There is breathing,
I am nothing but breath,
Breath is in me,
I breathe."

III. Contact

"The breath touches the nostrils as I breathe out."
"The breath touches the nostrils as I breathe in."

10 times

II. Think of the Course

"I breathe out, up from the navel,

[1] The Tetrad 2nd V. Feeling Joy, etc. From this stage on, the image is the object of concentration to be kept in mind while meditating.

through the thorax,
and out through the nostrils."
"I breathe in, through the nostrils,
through the thorax,
as far down as the navel."

I. Counting

"I breathe out a short breath."⎫
"I breathe in a short breath." ⎬ 10 times

"I breathe out a long breath."⎫
"I breathe in a long breath." ⎬ 10 times

Recite Ti Saraṇa.

SUTTA 118. MAJJHIMA NIKĀYA

O monks, this concentration on "mindfulness [1] as to respiration" being developed, peaceful and sublime, pure (undiluted), giving happiness, suppresses all ill and every immoral state that arises.

And how, O monks, is this concentration on mindfulness as to respiration developed? How being repeated, peaceful, sublime, undiluted, bestowing happiness, can it suppress all ill and every immoral state that arises? In this way ("here"), O monks. A monk, having reached the forest or the foot of a tree or a solitary place, sits down, crossing his legs, keeping the

[1] Attentive observation of respiration.

body straight, fixing his attention in front of him.[1]

Consciously he breathes out,
consciously he breathes in.

1. In breathing out a long breath he thinks (knows):
      "I breathe out a long breath."
   In breathing in a long breath he thinks:
      "I breathe in a long breath."

2. In breathing out a short breath he thinks:
      "I breathe out a short breath."
   In breathing in a short breath he thinks:
      "I breathe in a short breath."

3. "Conscious of the whole volume of breath I shall
      breathe out."
   "Conscious of the whole volume of breath I shall
      breathe in."

Thus he trains himself.

4. "Calming the whole volume of breath I shall
      breathe out."
   "Calming the whole volume of breath I shall
      breathe in."

Thus he trains himself.

5. "Feeling joy I shall breathe out."[2]

1 Looking toward the nose-tip.
2 Conscious of Joy.

"Feeling joy I shall breathe in."

Thus he trains himself.

6. "Feeling happiness I shall breathe out."
"Feeling happiness I shall breathe in."

Thus he trains himself.

7. "Conscious of the whole process of thought I shall breathe out."
"Conscious of the whole process of thought I shall breathe in."

Thus he trains himself.

8. "Calming the whole process of thought I shall breathe out."
"Calming the whole process of thought I shall breathe in."

Thus he trains himself.

9. "Observing (examining) the mind I shall breathe out."
"Observing the mind I shall breathe in."

Thus he trains himself.

10. "Gladdening the mind I shall breathe out."
"Gladdening the mind I shall breathe in."

Thus he trains himself.

11. "Concentrating the mind I shall breathe out."
    "Concentrating the mind I shall breathe in."

Thus he trains himself.

12. "Liberating (freeing) the mind I shall breathe out."
    "Liberating the mind I shall breathe in."

Thus he trains himself.

13. "Discerning impermanence I shall breathe out."
    "Discerning impermanence I shall breathe in."

Thus he trains himself.

14. "Conscious of the absence of passions I shall breathe out."
    "Conscious of the absence of passions I shall breathe in."

Thus he trains himself.

15. "Conscious of the cessation of all personal desires I shall breathe out."
    "Conscious of the cessation of all personal desires I shall breathe in."

Thus he trains himself.

16. "Conscious of the total absence of all personal desires I shall breathe out."

"Conscious of the total absence of all personal desires I shall breathe in."

Thus he trains himself.

EXTRACTS FROM CHAPTER VIII, 9TH DIVISION, OF THE PATH OF PURITY

VISUDDHI-MAGGA [1]

RÉSUMÉ

A monk having performed all his duties, having got rid of the hindrances, should rejoice his heart by calling to mind the Three Gems: the Buddha, the Dhamma, the Saṅgha.

His attention should then be concentrated upon the subject of meditation, "mindfulness as to respiration."

He should fix his attention upon the counts, the course, the contact (of the breath), and withdraw his attention from all conditioned and perishable things. Having understood their dissolution, he obtains the fruit of purification, he reflects upon all this.

ĀNĀPĀNA SATI

Practice-Plan (for practising the complete meditation)

Begin by reciting the short Love-formula—

---

[1] A new translation, including the principal comments of Buddha-ghosa, with practical explanations.

METTĀ

Saying:

"May I be happy, may I be free from all suffering;
may I keep my happiness and live without enmity."

Send loving thoughts to all sentient beings,

> High or low,
> Big or little,
> Weak or strong,
> Near or far,
> Visible or invisible.

Saying:

"May they be happy, free from all suffering;
may they preserve their happiness, and live without
enmity."

Meditate on the virtues of the Triple Gem—

TI SARAṆA

Buddhaṁ saraṇaṁ gacchāmi—think of intelligence
and compassion, as characteristics of the Buddha.

Dhammaṁ saraṇaṁ gacchāmi—think of the transcendental qualities of the Dhamma.

Saṅgham saraṇaṁ gacchāmi—think of the qualities of
those who follow the Four Higher Paths.

THE FIRST TETRAD

I

COUNTING—GANAṆĀ

Kaya (Body)

Breathe through the nose with the mouth shut.

Concentrate on and observe the counts, think of
 nothing else.

Dīghaṁ passasāmīti. . . .

"Consciously I breathe out a long breath."

  (counting 1 2 3 4 5 slowly).

Dīghaṁ assasāmīti. . . .

"Consciously I breathe in a long breath."

  (counting 1 2 3 4 5 slowly).

II

Rassaṁ passasāmīti. . . .

"Consciously I breathe out a short breath."

  (counting 1 2 3 4 5 quickly).

Rassaṁ assasāmīti. . . .

"Consciously I breathe in a short breath."

  (counting 1 2 3 4 5 quickly).

III

THE COURSE OF THE BREATH (ANUBANDHANĀ)

Follow then the *course* of the breathing. Discard counting from now on—follow from the nostrils through the chest and as far as the navel—return from the navel up through the chest and the nostrils, observing the breathing; so train oneself.

Sabbakāyapatisaṁvedī assasissāmīti. . . .

"Conscious of the whole volume of breath I shall breathe out." [1]

Sabbakāyapatisaṁvedī assasissāmīti. . . .

"Conscious of the whole volume of breath I shall breathe in."

IV

CONTACT—PHUSANĀ

Passambhayaṁ kāyasaṁkhāraṁ. . . .

"Calming the whole volume of breath I shall breathe out."

"Calming the whole volume of breath I shall breathe in."

---

[1] "Experiencing (or feeling) the whole body" means feeling the breath, in high, middle, and lower breathing.

The breathing has become tranquil and subtle—one is conscious of the breath striking the upper lip or nostrils. This *contact* is the *object of concentration*. Think only of the contact and not of the breath.

Now that the breathing has become so subtle, a sign or mental image of the breath arises.[1] Its appearance varies: some see it as having the colour and form of a spider's web, others see a mist, a bubble, a cloud, etc.

This image should now become the object of concentration. Pay attention to it without analysing the details, the surroundings, colour, etc.

THE SECOND TETRAD

V

Pītipaṭisaṁvedī. . . .
"Feeling joy I shall breathe out."
"Feeling joy I shall breathe in."

In the First and Second Jhānas one feels rapture and yet clearly knows that rapture is destructible and perishable; the joy of one who begins to understand the higher knowledge and to rid himself of what is inferior. But this rapture, being impermanent, is not the goal.

[1] Paṭibhāga Nimitta.

VI

Sukhapaṭisaṁvedī. . . .

"Feeling happiness I shall breathe out."

"Feeling happiness I shall breathe in."

That state of physical and mental well-being (happiness) which is experienced in the First, the Second, and the Third Jhānas.

Citta (Mind)

VII

Cittasaṁkhārapaṭisaṁvedī. . . .

"Conscious of the whole process of thought I shall
    breathe out."

"Conscious of the whole process of thought I shall
    breathe in."

As in all the four Jhānas one is conscious of the mind at work. The aggregates of mind are the sentiments and the understanding.

VIII

Passambhayaṁ cittasaṁkhāraṁ. . . .

"Calming the whole process of thought I shall breathe
    out."

"Calming the whole process of thought I shall breathe
    in."

Calming all the perceptions and feelings that are stored up in the mind, discerning these feelings, causing the lower mental states to cease, purifying the mind as in all the four Jhānas (where each stage leads to a subtler state of consciousness).

THE THIRD TETRAD

IX

Cittapaṭisaṁvedī. . . .

"Observing (examining) the mind I shall breathe out."

"Observing (examining) the mind I shall breathe in."

Observing the working of the mind, seeing how it becomes more and more concentrated in meditation and also in the four Jhānas.

X

Abhippamodayaṁ cittaṁ. . . .

"Gladdening the mind I shall breathe out."

"Gladdening the mind I shall breathe in."

Through concentration and insight the mind is gladdened, joyful as in the First and the Second Jhānas, but one observes that this joy is perishable, since it is impermanent; therefore this is not the goal.

XI

Samādaham cittam. . . .
"Concentrating the mind I shall breathe out."
"Concentrating the mind I shall breathe in."

Bringing the mind to one-pointedness so that it can think only of one object at a time.

XII

Vimocayam cittam. . . .
"Liberating (freeing) the mind I shall breathe out."
"Liberating (freeing) the mind I shall breathe in."

Saying: "I am free from the hindrances—lust, anger, sloth, restless broodings, doubts—as one is free in the First Jhāna."

Abandoning analysis and reflection, the sensation of joy, the sensation of happiness.

Freeing the mind from the perception of permanence by the perception of impermanence.

Freeing the mind from the perception of happiness by realizing the impermanence of happiness.

Freeing the mind from the perception of self by realizing selflessness.

Observing impermanence in all that constitutes the "self."

THE FOURTH TETRAD

XIII

Aniccānupassī. . . .

"Discerning (conscious of) impermanence I shall breathe out."

"Discerning (conscious of) impermanence I shall breathe in."

One should discern (observe) impermanence in all things and in oneself, the discerner. All things are in process of becoming and of dissolution.

XIV

Virāgānupassī. . . .

"Conscious of the absence of passions I shall breathe out."

"Conscious of the absence of passions I shall breathe in."

One is conscious of the advantages of these states of mind which arise when passions have been extinguished. Such states lead to insight and to the destruction of rebirths. There are two kinds of dispassion: (1) the dispassion temporarily obtained during meditation; (2) the absolute dispassion of Nibbāṇa; this is the goal.

XV

Nirodhānupassī. . . .

"Conscious of the cessation of all personal desires I
shall breathe out."

"Conscious of the cessation of all personal desires I
shall breathe in."

The desires born of the false notion of a "self."

XVI

Paṭinissaggānupassī. . . .

"Conscious of the absence of all personal desires I
shall breathe out."

"Conscious of the absence of all personal desires I
shall breathe in."

Renouncing desire for all conditioned things, phenomenal states, etc. Knowing that desire is totally
absent. Faring on toward Nibbāṇa.

BIBLIOGRAPHY

Ānāpāna Sati, by Dr. Cassius Pereira. Bastian, Colombo, Ceylon.

Acvaghosha's Discourse on the Awakening of Faith in the Mahāyāna, tr. Teitaro Suzuki. Open Court Publishing Co., Chicago, 1900.

Buddhist Manual of Psychological Ethics, tr. from the 1st Book of Abhidhamma Pitaka—Dhamma-Sangani (compendium of states of phenomena), by C. Rhys Davids, D.Litt., M.A. Royal Asiatic Society, London, 1923.

Compendium of Philosophy, tr. of *Abhidhammasattha-Sangaha* by Shwe Zan Aung, B.A., revised by Mrs. Rhys Davids, D.Litt., M.A. Oxford University Press, 1929.

The Expositor (Atthāsalinī); Commentary on the Dhammasangani, the 1st Book of Abhidhamma Pitaka, tr. by Maung Tin, M.A., Vols. I and II. Pāli Text Society, 1920–1.

The Fruit of the Homeless Life (The Sāmaññaphala Sutta), tr. Bhikkhu Sīlācāra. Buddhist Society of Great Britain and Ireland, 1917.

An Introduction to Yoga, by Claude Bragdon. Alfred A. Knopf, New York, 1933.

Introduction to the Essential Principles of the Dhamma, by Bhikkhu Sīlācāra.

Le Modernisme Bouddhiste et le Bouddhisme du Bouddha, by A. David. Alcan, Paris, 1911.

Majjhima Nikāya, ed. Pāli Text Society. London, 1899.

Manual of a Mystic (Yogāvacara's Manual), tr. F. L. Woodward, M.A., ed. Pāli Text Society. London, 1916.

Nature of Consciousness, by E. R. Rost, I.M.S., O.B.E., K.I.H., M.R.C.S., L.R.C.P. Williams & Norgate, Ltd., London, 1930.

On the Divine States, the 9th Chapter of the *Visuddhi-Magga* of Buddhaghosa, tr. C. Rhys Davids, D.Litt., M.A. Buddist Society of Great Britain and Ireland, London, 1921.

The Path of Purity, tr. of Buddhaghosa's *Visuddhi-Magga* by Pe Maung Tin. M.A., B.Litt., Vols. I and II. Pāli Text Society, 1923–9.

The Wisdom of the Aryas, by Bhikkhu Ananda M. (Allan Bennett). E. P. Dutton & Co., New York, 1923.

The Word of the Buddha, by Bhikkhu Nyānatiloka Thero, tr. by

Bhikkhu Sīlācāra. Buddhist Society of Great Britain and Ireland, London, 1907.

Yoga as Philosophy and Religion, by Surendranath Dasgupta, M.A., Ph.D. E. P. Dutton & Co., New York, 1924.

PĀLI TERMS

Abhidhamma	The metaphysical section of the Buddhist Canon.
Abhiñña	Psychic powers, "supranormal intellection." *Vide* Chapter 7.
Āhāro	Food, nourishment.
Ahiṃsa	Harmlessness toward all living beings, non-violence.
Ākāsa	Air, sky, space.
Ānāpāna	Inhaled and exhaled breath.
Anattā	Egolessness. There is no fixed unchanging entity to be found anywhere.
Anicca	Impermanence, transitoriness.
Anubandhanā	That which connects or follows.
Anussati	Remembrance, recollection, mindfulness.
Appamaññā	Boundless, immeasurable, applied to the perfect exercise of Love, Compassion, Sympathy, and Equanimity.
Appanā	Fixing of thought on an object.
Āsana	Sitting down, a seat, throne, position.
Asubha	Impure, ugly, nasty.
Bhāvanā	Developing by means of thought; meditation.
Bhikkhu	A Buddhist mendicant monk, one who has gone forth from home to homelessness and received ordination.
Bodhi	Supreme knowledge latent in the mind. It is constituted by the seven elements of enlightenment.
Bodhisatta	A being destined to attain fullest enlightenment or Buddhahood. A Bodhisatta passes through many existences and many stages of progress before the last birth, in which he fulfils his great destiny.
Brāhmaṇa	A man leading a pure, sinless, and ascetic life, often even synonymous with Arahat.
Brahmavihāra	Sublime or divine state of mind. There are four

	such divine states: Mettā, Karuṇā, Muditā, Upekkhā.
Citta	The heart (psychologically); i.e., the centre and focus of man's emotional nature as well as that intellectual element which inheres in and accompanies its manifestations—i.e., thought. The seat of intuition.
Dhamma	That which forms a foundation and upholds. The Dhamma or world-wisdom philosophy of the Buddha as contained and expounded in the Five Nikāyas. The Law or the Teaching.
Dukkha	Any bodily or mental state of dis-ease, irritability, etc.
Ekaggatā	One-pointedness of mind, as it is concentrated upon a single subject to the exclusion of every other idea.
Gaṇanā	Counting.
Indriya	Strength, faculty.
Jhāna	Meditation, a special religious experience reached in a certain order of mental states.
Kāmāvacara	The world of pleasure, the domain of the senses.
Kamma	The doing, deed, work. Action and the result of action.
Kammaṭṭhāna	Occasion or ground for contemplation. Term referring to the forty subjects of meditation given in the *Visuddhi-Magga*.
Karuṇā	Pity, compassion. The second of the Four Divine States.
Kasiṇa	Object or process by means of which mystic meditation may be induced, a device or artifice.
Kāya	Group, collection; body, volume.
Kāyasaṅkhāra	Usually translated the aggregates of the body. Sometimes meaning the volume of breath contained in the body. M.N. 118 and M.N. 44.
Khandha	In the collective sense: "All that is comprised under"; in the individual sense: "constituent element." Five sensorial aggregates condition the appearance of life.
Kusala	Clever, good, meritorious.
Loka	Visible world or sphere of creation.
Lokiya	Belonging to the world, general, worldly.

Lokuttara	Supramundane, transcending the world.
Magga	Way, foot-path.
Mettā	Love, goodwill (the first of the Four Divine States).
Muditā	Sympathy (with happiness). The third of the Four Divine States.
Nāma	Name (as a metaphysical term is opposed to Rūpa and comprises the four immaterial factors of an individual).
Nibbāṇa	Extinction of the fires of greed (lobha), ill will (dosa), and ignorance (moha); beyond the phenomenal plane, a state which may be attained even in this world.
Nimitta	Sign, omen, characteristic, image.
Nirodha	Cessation, suppression, destruction, annihilation (of sense-consciousness).
Nīvaraṇa	Hindrance, obstacle in an ethical sense.
Padhāna	Exertion, energetic effort, concentration of mind.
Paññā	Intelligence comprising all the highest faculties of cognition. Wisdom.
Parikamma	Arrangement, preparation.
Pārisuddhi	Purity, perfection.
Paṭibhāga	Likeness.
Patipassana	Reflection.
Phala	Fruit.
Phusanā	Touch, contact.
Piṭaka	Basket, term used for the three great divisions of the Pāli Canon: Ti Piṭaka, the three baskets or containers of tradition.
Pīti	Joy, delight.
Rūpa	Form, appearance, principle of form.
Sallakkhaṇā	Discernment, testing.
Samādhi	Concentration, intent state of mind and meditation which, concomitant with right living, is a necessary condition to the attainment of higher wisdom and emancipation.
Samaṇa	A recluse, a monk who has not yet received full ordination.
Samāpatti	Attainment. Four Rūpa-Jhānas and four Arūpa-Jhānas make up the eight attainments.
Samatā	Equality.

Sāmatha	Calm, quietude of heart.
Sammā	Perfect, true, best.
Saṁsāra	The perpetual wandering.
Saṅkappa	Thought, purpose, intention.
Saṅkhāra	Constituent, combination, aggregate.
Saññā	Sense, perception (the third Khandha).
Sarana	Refuge, protection.
Sati	Mindfulness, self-possession, intentness of mind, attention.
Satta	A living being, a sentient being.
Sīla	Morality. Purity of word, thought, and deed, including harmlessness to all beings.
Sotāpanna	A stream-winner, one who has entered the Path and freed himself of three fetters.
Sukha	Agreeable, pleasant; happiness.
Taṇhā	Thirst for existence, desire born of ignorance, craving, attachment to sense objects.
Ṭhapana	To place, to set up.
Theravāda	The Doctrine of the Elders, the Southern school of Buddhism.
Ti	Three. Threefold as applied to the Triple Gem— the Buddha, the Dhamma, the Saṅgha.
Uggaha	Acquiring, taking notice.
Upacāra	Approach, vicinity.
Upanibandhanā	Closely connected with.
Upasama	Peace, tranquillity.
Upekkhā	Equanimity, serenity.
Vacī	Speech, words.
Vavatthāna	Arrangement, fixing, that which occurs.
Vāyāma	Effort, endeavour.
Vedanā	Feeling, sensation. The second of the five Khandhas.
Vicāra	Investigation with the characteristic of movement, examination, consideration.
Viññāṇa	Intelligence, consciousness. The fifth of the five Khandhas.
Vipassanā	Inward vision, insight, intuition.
Viriya	Vigour, energy, exertion.
Visuddhi	Brightness, excellency, *purity*, rectitude.
Vitakka	Thought, investigation with the characteristic of fixity.

PĀLI TERMS

Yoga	That which joins together; to a Buddhist it is Discipline.
Yogāvacara	One who practises Yoga and spiritual exercises, the aspirant.

MORE TITLES ON BUDDHISM
FROM PILGRIMS PUBLISHING

www.pilgrimsbooks.com

For Catalog and more Information Mail or Fax to:

PILGRIMS BOOK HOUSE
Mail Order, P. O. Box 3872, Kathmandu, Nepal
Tel: 977-1-4700919 Fax: 977-1-4700943
E-mail: mailorder@pilgrims.wlink.com.np